Why Think?

A companion website to accompany this book is available online at:
http://education.stanley.continuumbooks.com

Whenever you see this icon, please type in the URL above to receive your
unique password for access to the book's online resources, which include the
Concept cards, Same Different cards and Fairy Tale Character cards, along with
many more printable resources for you to use in your lessons.

Further resources are available on the author's own website
www.childrenthinking.co.uk, and at www.p4c.com.

If you experience any problems accessing the resources, please contact
Continuum at: info@continuumbooks.com

Also available from Continuum

But Why?, Sara Stanley
The If Machine, Peter Worley
Teaching Thinking (3rd edition), Robert Fisher
Getting the Buggers to Think (3rd edition), Sue Cowley

Why Think?

Philosophical Play
from 3 to 11

Sara Stanley

continuum

Continuum International Publishing Group

The Tower Building   80 Maiden Lane
11 York Road   Suite 704
London SE1 7NX   New York NY 10038

www.continuumbooks.com

© Sara Stanley, 2012

British Library Cataloguing-in-Publication Data
A catalogue record for this book is available from the British Library.

ISBN: 978-1-4411-9360-5 (paperback)
        978-1-4411-6753-8 (ePub)
        978-1-4411-8365-1 (PDF)

Library of Congress Cataloging-in-Publication Data
Stanley, Sara.
  Why think? : philosophical play from 3-11 / Sara Stanley.
    p. cm
Includes bibliographical references and index.
ISBN 978-1-4411-9360-5 – ISBN 978-1-4411-6753-8 –
ISBN 978-1-4411-8365-1
  1. Philosophy–Study and teaching.   2. Education, Primary–Activity programs.   3. Games in philosophy education.   I. Title.
B52.5.S68 2012
372.3–dc23

                            2011046918

Typeset by Newgen Imaging Systems Pvt Ltd, Chennai, India
Printed and bound in India

Contents

List of Activities

List of Case Studies and Examples

Acknowledgements

Thanks to the children, parents, staff and governors of Sparhawk Infant & Nursery School, Norwich, who have made the last 3 years such a delightful and thoughtful experience. To the Year 5s at Acle Primary School, Norfolk and North Lakes School, Cumbria, who are proof that Philosophy works.

This book would, of course, not have been possible without them and especially my valued, inspirational and supportive colleagues Maria Cornish and Martyn Soulsby, and finally thanks to my family for their love and support.

With thanks for permission Marianne Lind

About the Author

Sara Stanley graduated with a BEd (Hons) from Homerton College, Cambridge, in 1997 where she specialized in drama and children's literature. She is a Foundation Stage Leader and full time nursery practitioner in Norwich. Her teaching is characterized by the development of philosophical skills through philosophical play, analysis of children's story telling and enquiry-based role play.

In addition, her teaching is constructed and led by the children through the use of quality picture books to develop thematic learning, philosophical understanding and enquiry. She is a Level 1 trainer with SAPERE (Society for Advancing Philosophical Enquiry and Reflection in Education).

Sara has also written several guides for the *Read and Respond* series, and is a keynote speaker both nationally and internationally on the subject of philosophical play and the development of critical thinking skills in the Early Years.

Introduction

Early attitudes to philosophical thinking and learning

Philosophy for Children, or P4C, as it will be referred to in this book, is a method of introducing philosophical thinking into the child's curriculum. We are all philosophers at heart. Philosophy is a method of thinking, reasoning and making sense of arguments and counterarguments.

We all philosophize at various times in our lives and perhaps more so as we are growing up. We want to know about our existence, our relationships, our place within society and the wider world. Philosophy is about asking important questions and trying to justify our answers. It is about asking questions and questioning theories that are relevant to our lives now, in the past and in the future. Adults and children alike have an innate desire to investigate and make sense of the world around us, what happens to us, how and why. The P4C method offers a practical, usable and exciting way of encouraging children to unlock their curiosity. By teaching them philosophical skills, you will provide children with the tools for genuine enquiry.

The aim of introducing P4C to very young children is to create a climate where independent thinking becomes the norm. As well as preschool being about play, making friends, getting messy with paint and play dough, it is also about talking and listening and thinking about tricky things. We want our parents to be asking not just 'what did you do today?' but also 'what did you hear, what did you talk about, what did you think about?'

Why Think? aims to allow practitioners to create such a climate through the provision of play-based games, thinking scenarios and activities, which have all been tried and tested. It also illustrates how to structure philosophical thinking from first observations of play and children's storytelling to full enquiries using picture books. The end of each chapter will offer questions or statements that are designed to allow time for personal reflection. These are questions we need to ask ourselves as classroom practitioners and philosophers who will be working with the children in future enquiries. By thinking about and utilizing these ideas, it will be possible to create and develop a classroom environment where books, philosophical adventure and storytelling are paramount.

Children's literature was the passion I first brought to my teaching career. When I had my first class of 5-year-olds, I realized that not only were books crucial to the creative, social and emotional education of our children but they also brought to the fore many unanswered questions. Books have the power to help children make sense of the world. These books become the vehicle for children to expand the concrete into the abstract and P4C becomes the tool which helps us work together towards understanding why these questions exist.

Throughout the book, I use the words, thoughts and questions of children from the Early Years Foundation Stage (EYFS), ages 3–5 years, to Key Stage 2, ages 7–11 years, to highlight the development of language, experience and conceptual understanding. These words have been left exactly as they were spoken to ensure that the children's characters, personalities and precise meanings are a true representation of their play and philosophizing. It is important that we as facilitators allow these words to always remain in the ownership of the child without adult 'translation'.

The worked examples of the children's dialogues form the backbone of the book; these illustrate the children's ideas, the facilitator's (your) interventions and the wide range of resources that are available to encourage philosophical discussion.

The most exciting thing about any classroom is the 'buzz'. The atmosphere of curiosity and engagement with learning that happens in a classroom, where children are encouraged to take ownership of thoughts and ideas, where their voices are not only listened to and respected but also challenged. This is what philosophy can do for a class of learners. Imagine being part of a class that loves to respond to and ask questions, such as 'who would we be if we swapped brains with our friend?' or 'how do we know that when we are asleep we are not all having the same dream?' Or maybe wondering whether computers could ever take over the world?

This is the sort of class we dream of – where children work together to puzzle over life's greatest philosophical mysteries, where they build confidence, respect and the ability to be reasonable and reasoned.

Philosophical teaching

The P4C movement started in the 1960s with Matthew Lipman. His vision was to encourage our young children to learn the art of reasoning, both to reason and be reasoned with. This approach to developing children's critical thinking skills is now practised in many countries worldwide. In the 1970s, Matthew Lipman and Ann Sharp produced a curriculum called Philosophy for Children based on the belief that children can and should be encouraged to philosophize. They were influenced by the Socratic method of starting from the point of knowing nothing and building an argument based on reasoning through agreement and disagreement. Socrates likened this method of dialogue to the 'giving birth of our ideas'.

Lipman and Sharp devised a programme where children were encouraged to talk and listen to each other within a community of enquiry, facilitated but not controlled by the teacher. Lipman wrote a series of philosophical texts to use with children. These texts explored among other things the big issues of morality, power, love, religion and the nature of our existence. He founded the institute for the advancement of philosophy for children based at Montclair State University in America. In 1992, the BBC made a television documentary titled *Socrates for Six-Year-Olds* based on the work of Lipman in New Jersey. This attracted a great deal of interest, and Dutch philosopher, counsellor and educator Karin Murris went to train with Lipman. She developed his methods by using picture books so that philosophy could be accessed by much younger children and without the added costs of expensive and difficult-to-find resources. It is now estimated that more than 50 countries worldwide use the P4C method.

The work in this book has developed from the foundations established by Karin Murris, Roger Sutcliffe and Joanna Haynes, under whom I trained. As an Early Years practitioner, my work focuses on breaking down the skills young children need in order to fully access the philosophical enquiry process.

Citizenship and the critical thinker

In a curriculum that is content and knowledge driven, it is important that our children know how to use acquired knowledge and look deeply into the understanding of their answers.

Knowledge is meaningless without this understanding, and what better way to understand than to talk and listen critically with peers.

P4C gives our young learners a chance to listen and talk within the safe structure of a 'dialogue'. At first this dialogue is facilitated by the adult who helps them formulate their ideas, listen to the ideas of others and question their way towards understanding. We aim for the children to become facilitators themselves. Soon, they will begin to make connections and explore unexpected possibilities. The philosophical setting provides the necessary ingredients for developing self-esteem, self-motivation and self-challenge. It is through this total immersion and engagement that the child begins to hear his or her own voice and understands what it is truly saying. Most importantly, it offers a framework for approaching other problems, both in their education and their wider experiences as citizens of a big society.

A philosophical approach to life is often mistaken to mean that people are sedentary and/or cerebral. This is not what I believe. P4C to me, and I hope what you will also see from the case studies in this book, is the production of wildly opposing positions and argument. It gives children the chance to change their mind through hard evidence. It is a plea for rationalism, not 'think this' but 'why think this?'

We need to encourage our children to be active, reactive, constructive, combative and creative. P4C is a rational and humane way of dealing with the world and we need to give our children a thirst to understand how they go about thinking rationally in a complicated world.

Giving children a voice

The P4C movement has long recognized and used Matthew Lipman's vision from the 1960s as a foundation for creating an educational tool that gives our children a voice not just in school but also in life.

Philosophy allows children to make connections with real-life experiences and gives them the confidence to test their ideas and questions about the complexities of the world in which we live. Philosophical teaching and learning requires curiosity about life's big questions. It is about building the foundations for children to reason effectively, and by doing so, begin to understand more about themselves and the world in which they live. It involves the exploration of philosophical themes, such as friendship, fairness, authority, power, justice, truth and knowledge. Questions that arise in the classroom and playground might start with 'Why doesn't my friend want to play with me?'; 'Why do I have to share?' or 'Is it always wrong to retaliate when I feel hurt or angry?' The answers to these questions are never as flippant or straightforward as 'because I said so'. Allowing children to discuss these issues empowers them to understand and resolve their own problems and dilemmas. Should adults have the right to choose working partners for our children? Should we force them to allow a left out child to play? What about the rights of the other child? Maybe it is only a game for one?

Children should be taught and encouraged to ask questions that challenge behaviours and scenarios of play. 'Why didn't I get a turn?' is an ideal opportunity to discuss the concept of fairness. 'He won't play with me' presents the chance for dialogue about friendship and the rights of the individual child.

When we ask our children to listen to each other, we must also accept that we, in turn, need to listen to our children too. We must take their fears and questions seriously. We should ensure that they have the opportunity to give these thoughts a voice in a safe and supportive environment where thinking is valued and championed.

This book will show how we can facilitate our children in their work and play from the earliest moments of their education. It will guide us through the progression and development of skills needed to become confident, logical, critical and challenging members of a community of enquiry.

The book will take us on a journey starting in the first weeks of a 3-year-old's education and accompany him or her to the gates of high school and life beyond the school system.

Our expectations of children, whatever age they start this philosophical journey, must remain consistent and vigilant. The activities and case studies in this book are relevant to children as young as 3 years of age, but are relevant or adaptable for children up to the age of 11 years as well. The outcomes, of course, will vary across age groups but will be equally enjoyable, accessible and valuable whatever the ages of the children.

P4C in the EYFS

Working in the EYFS with P4C is possibly one of the most challenging areas. Three- and 4-year-olds enter the philosophical curriculum with limited experiences and a lack of the expressive vocabulary necessary to articulate their ideas. It is therefore imperative that alongside the teaching of philosophical skills, the facilitator must ensure that there is overt modelling of the thinking processes. Practising teachers in the Early Years environment understand that young children need to access philosophy through the daily ethos of community questioning, reasonable reasoning and the sharing of ideas and opinions.

The Early Years teacher will be used to asking questions aloud in order to push for developmental learning in every area. Questions, such as 'I wonder what will happen if . . .'; 'Why does that happen?'; 'What do you think about this . . .', should already be commonplace in any excellent Early Years setting.

Philosophy in the Early Years involves bringing this questioning into the children's imaginative play. Working in this way has been influenced and inspired by Vivian Gussin Paley.

I do not ask the children to stop thinking about play. Our contract reads more like this: if you will keep trying to explain yourselves I will keep showing you how to think about the problems you need to solve. Vivian Gussin Paley
        – *Wally's Stories: Conversations in the Kindergarten*

It is imperative that children are involved in this enquiring and dialogic process from the earliest moments in their education. The modelling of early philosophical reasoning forms the basic framework for the more rigorous skills involved in P4C.

The P4C skill-based environment

P4C in the early years, or whatever age children begin the discipline, should focus on activities which:

- fine tune listening and speaking skills
- use the language of discussion
- enable pupils to think about similarities and differences between things
- allow pupils to ask questions and challenge the answers of their peers
- entitle pupils to vote and check that their thinking remains consistent
- encourage pupils to make a choice and give a valid reason for that choice
- empower children to explore both sides of an argument
- require pupils to share their thoughts and recognize that the opinions of others may differ from their own
- help pupils to turn statements into questions
- explore and develop an understanding of philosophical concepts.

These activities should be based around an exciting and accessible stimulus. Philosophy in the early stages should start with play and exploratory dialogue between adults and children. Many of the activities developed in this book are designed to engage pupils in a meaningful way within the context of story and imagination. Chapter 5, 'First Enquiries' (p. 102), will guide you through these early enquiries that aim to develop these skills.

For Chapters 1 and 2, practitioners will find it useful to build up a resource bank containing puppets, fairy tale figures, fairy tales, picture books and toys through which children can start exploring the simple concepts such as good and bad, right and wrong.

Chapters 4 and 5 will introduce early enquiries and encourage children to demonstrate their thought processes in a more structured, enquiry-based environment. At this stage, a set of basic concept picture cards and double-sided voting cards for children to use will be a useful resource. It is also helpful to have a set of building-block cards. These serve as reminders to the children of the skills they will be using in the session. Make these visually attractive and recognizable. We have provided photocopiable materials in these chapters and downloadable templates online but you may also wish to design your own.

The methodology of this book will encourage you to build in lots of drawing opportunities in the form of storyboards and illustrations of questions and ideas to explore as they come up in the Enquiry. Allow children to take ownership of these sessions by displaying these thinking pictures and sharing them with parents and carers.

It is ultimately the laying of these early philosophical stepping stones and skill-based building blocks that will pay dividends. The consolidation and confident application of these skills will enable pupils to bring logic, understanding and reasoning to their lives.

This book aims to inspire you as practitioners to create enquiries with your own classes of children. The case studies are not laden with heavy analysis of what happened and why but are aimed to help you think for yourselves about what is happening in the dialogues. Through hearing the words of real children and the connective facilitation that holds it all together, we can imagine the voices of our own children.

It is important that we realize that P4C is not just an educational theory but can produce real and tangible results. As practitioners, we need to realize what is possible with our own children and be inspired to put our children in the place of the children in this book.

1

Starting with Play

Why philosophy starts with play

We start with exploring the ways that children play. This play takes many forms, from tentative exploration to full-blown adventures. Children's play encompasses and consolidates everything they know and many more things that they do not yet know. They know that it involves love, concern and the conflict of family life. They know that monsters might be real. Their play involves the reliving of day-to-day experience but can swing quickly from the mundane re-enacting to the wildly fantastical. A shopping trip can transform with unstoppable speed into an encounter with fierce dragons.

In a young child's mind, the two realms of reality and fantasy are blurred yet irrevocably intertwined in the form of 'what do I know?' and 'what do I imagine?'

Children unlocking the doors to a world of play where anything is possible can be problematic.

If a Big Bad Wolf can blow the little pigs' house down, why can't I knock down the bricks my friends are playing with?

If we as adults do not take time to discover why conflict happens in the classroom, then we will be unable to communicate ways to solve future problematic situations. When we present this problem of the bashed down bricks to the children in story form, we allow them to judge the Big Bad Wolf, not the child. But all children are accessing a familiar problem and looking into the moral consequences of their play. What we are doing is helping to rebuild the connection between the children's imaginations and the real world.

All young mammals play, and this play is practice for future pack behaviour and indeed, survival. Our world seems sometimes to have disconnected from this view that play is necessary. Is this because if we do not see play seriously, play becomes 'childish'. If we can invite ourselves into the children's world of play, we can use it for the purpose nature intended: to make sense of the complicated maze of human behaviours, needs and emotions.

In the same way that lion cubs practice pouncing, our children are practicing moral and ethical positions – thinking about consequences of actions: Who is the strongest? Who is justified? Just because you can, does that mean you should?

Children are not necessarily conscious of this until it is pointed out to them in terms of what they already know and understand.

Taking time to understand a child's play can remove unnecessary and destructive labelling of the child who always seems to get it wrong. When we invite children into each other's play, it allows them to form cohesive interactions and creates an understanding of a whole spectrum of behaviours. There are numerous occasions in my classroom where adult interventions are required, times when adults provide the tools to deal with conflicts. We model language, such as 'excuse me, I haven't finished playing with that?' and 'please could I have it when you've finished?' for incidents that involve the sharing of equipment. But we also need to provide tools for more complex problems in play. For example, how do we deal with situations where children are refused entry into social cliques? Or dealing with situations where children's behaviours seem beyond the boundaries that others are prepared to accept? What happens when a child has too much power, or not enough?

These are the situations where adults can step in to examine play and allow the children to see play through the eyes and feelings of others.

Examples of solving conflict in play

Situation – Child refusing to say hello to the class at hello time

Poppy:	Why didn't James say hello?
Facilitator (F):	Why don't you ask him?
Poppy:	Why didn't you say hello? It makes me sad when you don't say hello
Holly:	It's not being a friend not to say hello
Sarah:	You can sit here
James:	No I don't like you
F:	Tell James how that makes you feel?
Sarah:	Sad
F:	Do you think James should say sorry and put things right or go and sit away from the circle for a while?
Poppy:	Sit away
Millie:	But we want him to be happy
F:	How would that happen?
Sarah:	If he says sorry to me
Jessica:	James could pretend to be Sarah
Cybele:	Yes, Sarah should let James be her then James will be sad like Sarah. Maybe on another day we can dress him up as Sarah?
Ryan:	If they have someone else's coat on they will be just like someone else
F:	Is that true? If you put Mrs Dawson's coat on would you be Mrs Dawson?
Ryan:	Yes
F:	James, would you like to be Sarah?
James:	No because I'm not feeling well
F:	If you had told us you were sad we could have helped couldn't we?
James:	Yes – Sorry Sarah
F:	Are you ready to say hello now?
James:	Yes, hello

Class responded with hello greeting

Situation – The mermaid clothes. I want, I'll have

I was working with a group of children when I heard Liam saying 'sorry, sorry' to Sophie

I intercepted Sophie as she flew past me, not upset but running. As I sat down with her to find out what had happened Liam arrived.

Liam:	I said sorry
F:	What happened? Why are you saying sorry?
Liam:	Because I said she was naughty to just take the mermaid clothes from Holly, she can't just snatch them
F:	Was Holly wearing them then?
Sophie:	Yes
F:	What could you have done then?
Liam:	She should have said can I have them when you've finished
F:	Is Liam right? Do you think he should be saying sorry or should you be saying sorry?
Sophie:	Me
F:	Who to?
Sophie:	Holly
F:	Maybe you should also say thank you to Liam for helping you remember the right choice
Sophie:	Thank you

She then took the clothes back to Holly. Three minutes later Sophie came to me

Sophie:	Holly has finished with them now so I am wearing them.

Both examples of dealing with conflict show that even with children as young as 3 years, we must encourage the child not only to take responsibility for his or her actions but to understand the impact his or her actions have on others. This social responsibility is a key area of development in philosophical thinking. In order that young children can partake in group enquiries, they must understand the connections between behaviour and consequence. Allowing time to unpack conflict instead of hurrying past it helps develop a sense of collective responsibility where children are encouraged not to 'tittle tattle' about each other but work together to find out why things happen and how they can be resolved; both these examples demonstrate that the children felt the need to resolve these issues with both fairness and compassion – a quality necessary for reasoned argument in future philosophical dialogues.

They are not sharing

One child came to me and complained that one child in the story area was not sharing the fairy tale characters.

I asked if this was something they needed help to work out.

They replied yes.

We resolved the issue to the point where both parties seemed able to continue their play in harmony. However, I wondered whether this was the true outcome one of the girls had wanted. I decided to present the situation to the class.

I asked the children to consider the following question:

F:	Are we allowed to play by ourselves in nursery?
	Chorus of 'No. We need to make friends.'
F:	Do all games have more than 1 person?
Ella:	If we want to play by ourself we can say you can play
F:	But what if it's a game for just one do you have to stop?
Poppy:	No it wouldn't be fair to you
Cybele:	If you finish your game then you can play with someone else
Holly:	Sometimes your mums and dads don't let you they make you go in your rooms and say play by yourself
F:	Is it good to play by yourself?
Poppy:	Yes I play by myself

F: Do you think it would be fair if I made you play with someone
            else if I saw you playing by yourself?
Cybele: I wouldn't like it
Millie: But I think it would be fair because you really do have to play or
            your friend will be angry
Harry: I think yes and no because sometimes you do want to be alone
            and sometimes not
F: What – If we had a rule that you had to play with any person,
            even if they are not one of your friends?
Millie: But we are all friends in nursery
F: We are here but what if you were somewhere else like at the
            park. If there were children there you didn't know and they
            were a bit rough?
Ryan: No you wouldn't like to play with children who do naughty things
Holly: I would make them as my friend by playing with them
Henry: I would tell them off or tell my mum and then they'd get in trouble
Millie: I would make them be good
F: How do you do that?
Millie: I don't know
F: Can you make people nice?
Poppy: Yes you make them laugh

This dialogue demonstrates that children are often in conflict between what they feel and what they are told is the right behaviour. From an early age, grown-ups try to instil a sense of right and wrong into their children. Young children are very perceptive, they know what they *should* do but it doesn't always seem fair. In this case, the children showed a developing awareness and understanding of both sides of the argument. Do we have to share our private games with others? Should we as adults force children into these situations? It is surely more productive to let the children discuss it, teaching them that it is alright to explain their preferences and reasons to other children without causing conflict?

The Early Years Foundation Stage (EYFS) is built almost entirely on the understanding that play builds knowledge. Children pretend in order to make sense of the world they experience. Play in the early years builds trust between children and the adults who interact with them because their play is taken seriously. When an adult offers encouragement, clarifies ideas and asks open questions with genuine interest, it supports and extends different pathways in thinking. This exploration of meaning behind role play and playful dialogue allows children to make concrete connections with their often abstract storylines.

In my classroom, all playful dialogues are recorded by an adult. Play is left as uninterrupted as possible. The adult becomes a silent participant in the game. What happens next is more powerful. The 'stories' are shared at story time. The dialogues are read out and questions are asked. 'What would have happened if?' 'Why was X cross about?' 'How did this or that happen?'

The children as a class comment on their play scenarios. They give reasons why characters behaved or spoke the way they did. The observer also now becomes a facilitator, modelling the desire to understand how play works. During the telling of the children's role-play stories, we explore through adult facilitation issues, such as power, truth, magic, friendship, equality, justice, good and bad, real and pretend.

Children begin to see connections not just between pretending to be somebody or doing something but why these issues arise and how they are relevant to real experiences they may encounter. Understanding play is play with real purpose. Below are some examples of role-play situations and stories and how they have been developed through adult and peer questioning, enquiry and dialogue.

Resolving philosophical conflict in role play

I have heard teachers say that certain children are not allowed in the role-play area or they close the role-play areas at certain time or even in some cases, do not have one in the classroom at all. The reasons given usually go along the lines of 'the children don't play properly in there'; 'it causes too many arguments' or 'I don't have time to keep sorting out the conflict in this space.'

In play, there is often a suspension of belief that teachers and children themselves can find frustrating, and it is this which often leads to conflict. In play, injustice is felt most often. Who chooses what happens in the play? Why is it not going the way different children want it to? Who plays which role? Why do the boys turn props into weapons? And ultimately, how and why do negotiations break down? By not allowing the children to experience conflict, we are not letting them explore and learn through the moral choices they make. From a very young age, we should expect our children to take responsibility for their actions. Play without consequence can block emotional learning. Play is at its most powerful when children are actively and emotionally learning. It is important that they learn that imaginary play has imaginary consequences. This is why recording dialogue and sharing it with the children can push the boundaries of what role play can achieve. Through discussion and enquiry about role play and conflict in role play, the children become morally culpable for their behaviours. We ask together 'why did that happen?' and 'Was it OK for that to happen?' In doing so, we are making our children aware of their moral behaviour within the safety of role play.

The castle and dungeon role-play area

A small group of children were playing in the castle role-play area. Ella came to me to tell me that some children were being silly in the castle.

Ella: 'They mustn't be pirate robbers'

I went with her to the role play area and asked the children whether they knew how to get rid of pirate robbers?

Ella: We put them in the real bin

Demi: No we'll put you in our real jail (*the children had designed and built a dungeon area into their castle when it was first made*)

Kennedy: Then you be naughty pirates

Tayla: Tell them off, say you naughty pirates

Demi: I am a baddie

Tayla: And I'm a goodie knight

Shauna: I'm a princess

Kennedy: I'm a King

Kennedy: Oh no the knight will kill her. Where's the king's crown? You can't be a king without a crown. People listen only if you got that crown

Tayla: It's too big

Kennedy: Come on let's steal all the treasure . . . oh no you don't come in our castle

Demi: Ha-ha! I'll take you to my pirate robber ship. No go in there because I'm a nice pirate it's a nice sleeping bed . . . ahaha I've trapped you got you

Demi: I am a queen called majesty

Kennedy: I thought you was a pirate?

Demi: I'm a queen that turned into a pirate

Kennedy: Mrs Stanley, we're trapped. Demi trapped us

Demi: I'm a pirate that's what they do

Ella:	Queen can you pretend me was a pirate? A fairy pirate?
Jessica:	who's the saver? You need a helper-stop; don't pull the door you're going to break it
Kennedy:	But how can we get out of this jail?
Ella:	I don't know, can we get out?
Jessica:	Go help Ella
Demi:	Make a drink, I'm going to make it poisonous and make them drink it
Jessica:	I think that game's not good. It's about bad stuff. My Nan who lives in London doesn't like scary stuff on telly, only football.
Kennedy:	Help us, help me. I'm getting cold
Tayla:	Stop it. Are you alright?
Kennedy:	Please can I come out now?
Demi:	No, go in
Kennedy:	Oh no, now she's king of the pirates
Demi:	Now, here's your dinner, eat that. It's very good
Shauna:	You have to drink it, no one's allowed out
Kennedy:	But where are we going to sleep in this dungeon? Where will I put my pretend cloak?
Shauna:	Demi, let me have some pretend tea
Ella:	Come out Kennedy, we're not shut in any more. We're not trapped. That naughty fairy let me out
Demi:	Shauna, Come help me no hold the door shut tight
Shauna:	The police is coming now to take them twins 'hello 999 Policemans?'
Demi (to Shauna):	You be king and wear the crown
Shauna:	No it's too big for me
Jessica:	I'm going to sort them out
Kennedy:	Can I come out for storytime on the grass?
Kennedy:	Yes . . . is everybody nasty here? Can I go play in the back garden King?
Demi:	No, only play here – I've got a letter, it says, 'from Demi'
Ella:	Can I have the fairy costume now?
Demi:	No, it's only mine, or shall I have this big one?
Kennedy:	Yes you have that big crown you can be our fairy Godmother
Demi:	Look in this mirror
Kennedy:	There's no one there
Kennedy:	I'm tired mummy can I go to bed?
Demi:	Yes I need to get you a pillow
Kennedy:	No not that one, it's too rough
Kennedy:	Oh morning time now, hurray

After sharing this dialogue with the children the most dominant reaction was that Demi was being mean.
   I asked the children why they thought that this was the case.

Jude:	Because she is in charge
F:	What does that mean?
Jessica:	It means it's her game so she can be the one in charge
Ella:	She is only playing tricks
F:	What tricks did she play?
Chloe:	Like when she gave them poison and locked them in the dungeon
Poppy:	But that was not nice
F:	Why did the others let her do that?
Kennedy:	Because it was a game and you have to do what people tell you in a game
F:	Does everyone agree with that idea?
Chloe:	No I think you can play your own game and go away
Henry:	But what if you are in the dungeon?
Ella:	Then you have to say let me out
F:	Is that still part of the game?
Kennedy:	Yes, if you have got a crown on but if you haven't then you say let me out
F:	So is it ok to be mean in a game?

Divided response

Buddy:	I think it is ok but not too mean
Jessica:	If it is a game then you say yes I can be mean
Poppy:	But you don't hurt people
Ella:	Sometimes people do hurt me in a game and I cry
F:	Is it possible that people forget they are playing a game?
Demi:	When you are playing a game you might hurt someone but it's not your fault
Kennedy:	Yes it's because you are pretending
F:	So if it's only a game is that allowed?

Again response is quite divided

Gemma:	No, because we can't hurt people
Buddy:	But if they are not playing right then you might need the crown and forget to ask
Chloe:	Mean people don't ask, they push
Buddy:	It's OK to push if you are wearing the crown but not if its too big or it isn't your turn
F:	Who decides who is the mean person in the game?
Chloe:	It is who says so

Ella:	If you are the baddie then you have to have a turn or if you are the goodie you can say please can I be the baddie now?
Demi:	Then the game won't be good because goodies are supposed to be goodies and not be mean
F:	Can baddies turn into goodies though?
Buddy:	If they say sorry they can

This dialogue focused the children on the boundaries of play and reality. Most children already know at the age of 3 years that hurting is not acceptable but there is still an obvious dichotomy in whether play counts as real life. Is this because they take their role as a character so seriously?

Common musings in the nursery environment

Real versus pretend

One of the most obvious areas of young children's development is their developing awareness of self. The early years are a time for exploring and discovering, who am I? Who are you? What is real? What is pretend? These are the boundaries that are crossed backwards and forwards throughout each day.

Where has the real me gone?

Below is a short dialogue that took place as a group of four 3-year-olds played dressing up. Here the children were exploring the difference between their real identities and the personas that they created when in costume.

Kennedy:	Where's the real me gone? I've lost her
Jessica:	I made her disappear, I'm a cheeky fairy
Kennedy:	Where is she? I'm not Kennedy anymore. I'm Princess Belle
Ella:	And I'm snow white lady. Ella has gone, my real Ella is gone.
Jessica:	I made all you disappear (giggles)
Kennedy:	I must find the real Kennedy, I'm worried . . . now I've lost my daddy now

(Kennedy changes out of her princess costume)

| Kennedy: | I'm back, I'm back it's me! |

(Ella does the same)

Ella:	Yeah it's me again
Ella:	Oh, Tayla has disappeared now
Jessica:	Whatever's going on? It's a magic day today.

I read this dialogue as a story to the children at the end of the day.

F:	So did the real Kennedy really disappear?
Sophia:	Yes she did 'cos she was a princess. Kennedy can't be a princess *and* a little girl can she?
F:	Can you still be you if you are pretending to be someone else?
Kennedy:	No, 'cos that's not how you play that game
Poppy:	Yes you can because she is only dressed up. She's still under her dress isn't she?
Chloe:	But she was talking in a princess voice
F:	So where did the girls go when they were dressed up?
Tayla:	They was in the house
Kennedy:	No we was on the carpet with Jessica wasn't we?
Jessica:	Yes we were here but my daddy was lost
Shauna:	Maybe you was lost too?
Jessica:	Yes I think I was lost
Shauna:	Don't put that Princess Belle dress on again will you.

The children here are exploring the true nature of identity. Can you still be yourself while playing at being someone else? Pretend play is vital in discovering who we are but what does it tell us about the philosophical idea of identity?

One child in the class came to nursery with tales of her pretend friends, Dap-Dap, Bor-Bor, Katy Cut and Fraser Bear. These characters and their adventures were often referred to in her first few months of nursery. Here I recorded a sample of her solitary play involving two of her imaginary friends.

Poppy:	I've put a tiger in the cage because he kept jumping on my tummy and there's a baby in there.
	It's been in there eight years, it's coming out in a minute – it's coming out at the Doctors. One of my pretend friends can be the Doctor, what about Dap-Dap? I'll lie down and pretend they cut my tummy open. That lady can be my baby. I'll hold it to my tummy 'look at my baby!' Now I'm a mummy I have to do her nappy. She's got a do-do, yuck! – I don't like them, only when they're in the toilet yes? Fraser Bear doesn't have pretend friends I put them away in the cupboard 'cos he keeps bashing them on the head'.

The children were very used to Poppy mentioning her imaginary friends and accepted them without question, in fact, in much the same way as other children had 'special' toys that came to nursery with them. I wondered whether the children really did understand the difference between imaginary and real. I used the example of Ellie, a special toy elephant bought daily to nursery by Millie.

I read the above dialogue to the class and asked whether anybody had seen Poppy's imaginary friends playing with her?

Most children replied no

Poppy:	That's because only I can see them
F:	How can we know what they look like?
Poppy:	That's because I can tell you or draw a picture
F:	Could you take a photograph of them with the camera?
Poppy:	Yes
F:	Does anyone think differently?
Jessica:	I think you can't 'cos we can't see them. We can see them if they are a picture
F:	So is the picture real then?
Millie:	Yes that's a real drawing and then that will be Poppy's friends
Harry:	No, paper is not real, it's only a drawing
F:	So how can Poppy's friends talk then?
Millie:	From their mouth
F:	So if they are not real can they have a real mouth?
Cybele:	No
F:	Millie, can your Ellie talk?
Millie:	Yes I can talk to Ellie and she can talk to me
F:	Can everyone hear Ellie?
Millie:	No, only my mummy hears her, not my sister
F:	We can see your Ellie but we can't see Dap-Dap. Are they both real?
Millie:	No, only Ellie is real
Poppy:	No, Dap-Dap is real 'cos he does naughty things but he is going to Africa soon and then we won't see him
F:	Will he still be real in Africa?
Poppy:	Yes but he is going to a funeral so we won't see him anymore

The following issue of bravery is often referred to in the nursery class. Children are becoming aware that there are elements of danger in their emerging worlds. They look for ways to deal with anxiety, often through story and, in particular, fairy tales. The children have a storytelling area in the classroom where they can access the fairy tale characters. This is a popular place to work out fear and test out bravery.

What is bravery?

A small group of children are playing with the fairy tale figures

Kelsey: Hello I'm a scary big bad wolf
Lucy: Hello I'm a scary red riding hood
Chloe: Hello I'm the good little piggies
Jessica: Ooh yum, I'm a big bad wolf
Kelsey: Help, there's a big bad wolf outside, oink oink! Help help!
Lucy: Be brave little piggies, be brave
Chloe: Quick, there's a monster
Lucy: Hello hello, I'm little red riding hood. Don't fright me, I'm not brave(r) enough

I read this play scene out to the children and asked them to think about how we could help Red Riding Hood be brave enough.

F: What do you think being brave means?
Jessica: I think it means stretch up
Millie: No, I think it's when we don't care about anything
Holly: When we just don't take any notice of the big bad wolf. I would just walk away
F: Is that being brave do you think?
Cybele: No I think being brave would be if you died the wolf
Holly: I had to be brave when I saw the Disney characters I didn't like them when I was three but now I'm not scared of anything

Millie: I had an operation on my eyes and had eye drops. I didn't really like them but I was brave

Jessica: I got a sticker for being brave at the dentist but I didn't have medicine

F: So why did you get a sticker then?

Jessica: I don't know

F: Were you being brave then?

Harry: No not really, you don't get stickers for doing nothing, only something

Poppy: Like at the library

Millie: Yes or the Doctors

Kelsey: I had a sticker at the doctors when I had my needle

Cybele: I did too. I was brave

F: What did it mean to be brave then?

Cybele: I had to not cry but I did

F: So did you get a sticker?

Cybele: Yes

F: But if you cried were you being brave?

Cybele: Yes I was brave I only cried 'cos it was hurting, but only a bit crying

F: What would you have done if you weren't brave?

Cybele: I wouldn't have let the doctor do it. I might cry and go away

Millie: But then your mum would be cross

F: Are you more scared of your mum or the doctor?

Millie: The doctor

F: So, Cybele, you were brave to let the doctor do that to you then?

Cybele: Yes

Harry: I am brave when I fall over

Jude: I'm brave when I'm bigger, like my daddy

Tyler: If there's a ghost you have to run away like Scooby doo. Scooby doo he isn't brave

Holly: I been on a bear hunt I'm brave I'm not scared of bears

F: What are you scared of?

Holly: Monsters

F: Why are people scared of monsters?

Millie: Because we don't see them and they say Boo

F: I wonder if things we see are scarier than things we don't see?

This dialogue shows how their perceptions of bravery flit seamlessly between the real and the imaginary worlds. If children do not yet know what is real, then how can they conceive what reaction they will have to an imaginary creature or situation? Allowing children to share their ideas about things that scare them offers new thoughts, ideas and often reassurance. It is important that their innate understanding of emotions, in this case fear, is not restricted to real scenarios. If we underestimate the capacity of their imaginations to induce fear, then we are not giving them the structure to deal with difficult emotions in the world. When a child plays at being Red Riding Hood confronted by the Big Bad Wolf, we are allowing them the opportunity to rehearse how fear and bravery may feel in the Big Bad World.

When children enter nursery at 3 years, they are told by their parents that they will make lots of friends. Often parents' main concerns are 'Does my child have any friends yet?' It is rare for children to be 'friendless' at this age because they are surrounded by companions. But they have not yet formed friendships in the way that adults understand friendship. Young children may still prefer observational or solitary play in line with their development but this does not mean they are lonely or 'friendless'. The word 'friend' is at this age often a generalization meaning 'children I encounter every day in my play'; when play goes wrong for a child, they will say 'you are not my friend any more.' When they are playing together and lost in the joy of the moment, they will say 'you are my best friend.' Best friends can be made and lost several times over and with several children over the course of a session. We also hear 'are you my friend?' from those children who are yet to make sense of this word and its puzzling, often contradictory nature. As a facilitator of children's thinking, I find that friendship is one of the most common themes to arise as the children grow, learn and mature together over the course of three or five terms in the nursery setting. I aim to ensure that this 'word' becomes a fertile ground for children to discuss how people should deal with each other and how they should behave themselves.

What are friends for?

Contextual information – three children are sitting at the table sorting buttons into tiny boxes.

Poppy: I have buttons at my home
Tyler: Do you do you live near school?
Poppy: Yes, would you like to come to my house?
Tyler: Yes
Poppy: You could come and play buttons at my house and sort them my dad cooks

Tyler: OK

(Another child, Millie, joins them at the table)

Millie: Look what I've done
Tyler: Wow that's a lot of writing
Millie: I know, I worked hard
Poppy: Well I work hard. I go to ballet class and I help my mummy tidy
           up, it's boring but it has to be done
Millie: Poppy can you help me with these buttons?
Poppy: OK that's what friends are for

Discussion: What are friends for?

I read out the snippet of dialogue and asked the children if they knew what Millie meant when she said 'that's what friends are for'

Holly: I've got a nice friend, she is for sharing
Kelsey: And to make you happy
Shana: And to play with each other
F: So what happens if they don't play with you?
Jude: Sometimes my friend plays with someone else and that makes
           me sad
Cybele: I think when people aren't nice to you then they are not your
           friend
Millie: If your friend is not nice you tickle them
Poppy: If they don't play, then they don't have to play with you all the
           time. *(pause)*
           Just sometimes
Kelsey: They don't play with you all the time
Harry: I think your friend could be cross with you but still be your friend
           another day
Holly: But that is sad
Millie: But I have a friend from another nursery who I only see
           sometimes
F: So what is it that makes her your friend if you don't play with
           her often?
Millie: I think it is my heart that says she is my friend
Poppy: I think inside my brain there is a heart and that tells me who to
           love and what my friend is
F: So if your friend moved far away they would still be in your
           heart?
Poppy: I think they can be there if you want them to be
F: If they were mean to you and you decided not to like them
           anymore, what happens then?

Tyler:	I think you take them out of your heart
Millie:	No I think they have to be there for always like your mum
Poppy:	But I had a friend when I was a baby and I don't even remember who
F:	So do we know what friends are for? Do we choose them?
Millie:	I think sometimes they choose us
Cybele:	Or our mum says you must be friends
F:	What about in nursery? Do we have to be friends?
Holly:	Yes because that's what school is we have to be good
F:	Do I tell you to be friends?
Group (*chorus*):	No
Millie:	But we like to be friends
F:	So you do choose then?
Millie (*and several other children*):	*Yes!*
F:	So how do you choose who can come to your party?
Kelsey:	Only you can have best friends and they can but not all your friends. That's too much
F:	How are best friends different?
Poppy:	They come to your house for tea
Millie:	And you wear the same nice dresses like this red one
Jessica:	But Ryan is my friend and he doesn't wear a dress

(Lots of laughter)

F:	Perhaps we can tell some more stories about friends to help us understand it better?
All:	Yes!

This dialogue shows that the children already understand there can be degrees of friendship. There is an awareness of affinity with others, 'We wear the same dresses,' and a knowledge that only best friends get to come to tea or come to parties. What it also conveys is the idea that friendship is mysterious. The children share many experiences and bond in the nursery setting where they understand the necessity for friendship but it is evident that they cannot find the words to describe the concrete attributes of friendship. However, they seem to know what it 'feels like'. They make reference to the emotions of sadness and joy and wonder whether it is the heart or brain that allows friendships to become real. These ideas are of course an early introduction into the philosophy of duality.

When does a child stop playing?

When does a child stop playing? Many would argue 'never'. As adults we still explore and experiment, fiddle and interact with media playfully. But for what purpose? For enjoyment?, to relieve stress?, to understand? When our Key Stage 2 National Curriculum refers only to 'work', what message are we sending to our seven plus year olds? Are we ever too old to have fun?

Throughout the EYFS, there is reference to thinking skills and opportunities for developing these skills through adult support and modelling, creating an effective learning environment and giving children enough time to develop their ideas. The revised EYFS Framework due to be implemented in September 2012 places emphasis on *how*, rather than *what* children should learn. Contained in the proposal guidelines for the revised EYFS Framework March 2011 under the heading 'Equipped for life, ready for school', Dame Clare Tickell states,

> I recommend that playing and exploring, active learning, and creating and thinking critically are highlighted in the EYFS as three characteristics of effective teaching and learning.

Within the Learning and Development theme, the two key principles, Active Learning and Creativity and Critical Thinking, support the notion of sustained shared thinking.

Active Learning has to involve other people, ideas and events that engage and involve children for sustained periods. It is through sustained, creative and thoughtful play with their peers and adults that shared progressive thinking can be developed. This thinking process takes time to develop which is why we must engage our youngest children in this from their earliest days.

Creativity and Critical Thinking – allowing children to explore and share their ideas through play in different situations and with a variety of resources – ensure that they discover connections and come to new, more meaningful and purposeful ways of doing and understanding things in the world around them. Dame Clare Tickell's EYFS framework report recognizes that adult support in this process 'enhances their ability to think critically and ask questions'.

Opportunities to promote the development of thinking skills within the EYFS are plentiful. In the key messages of the EYFS effective practice – *Play and Exploration* (2007) – it states that:

> children need to experience making mistakes in a safe environment, they need opportunities to test their ideas, to learn through play situations that they have chosen to explore. . . [In play] they share experiences and understandings, talk and thinking with the other children and the adults who join in the play and explorations.

The Key Stage 1 curriculum makes reference to the importance of role play in the development of literacy skills but there is little mention of play by the time our children reach Key Stage 2. It is worth remembering that the children in this Key Stage are still very young. In any culture, 7- to 11-year-olds are still very much children and surely deserve the right to play and be children, even in school? It seems to be up to our teachers to apply careful and creative interpretations of the strategies. Teachers of children in Key Stage 2 are mindful that these are still effectively young children. Even allowing opportunities for children to draw and illustrate their thinking brings an element of playfulness to learning. We must not lose sight that even adults need to play. Engaging in philosophical activities with our peers enables us not to lose sight of the joy of playing together with words, thoughts, ideas and even fantasies.

Reflecting on the nature of play and philosophy

- *At what age should we consider that play is childish?*
- *Do we ever stop playing?*
- *When does 'play' become work?*
- *Is all play good?*
- *Does play have to have a purpose?*
- *Can play exist without imagination?*

2
Storytelling and Fairy Tales

Starting with the children's stories

One of the most important things that we as facilitators of children's learning have to do is learn from the children. We need to be prepared to learn to listen to our children. We must listen with both attachment and detachment to the messages our children give. We attach to the meaning of their stories, attach to the glimpses of how they see themselves, their fears and dreams and puzzlements but we must also detach from the assumption that we know what these stories or conversations mean. We can, however, help children make sense of their stories by listening, by asking questions sensitively and by validating the creativity and purpose of storytelling.

Our children enter school with imaginations that need to make sense of the mysterious worlds they encounter: changing relationships, new friends, new places, new social situations and ever-changing rules. As facilitators, we must ensure that we take every opportunity to model listening skills. The best way to demonstrate that we listen is to repeat back and show interest in what our children say and why. They bring to the Early Years classroom a natural ability to create stories. What they might not bring is the language to communicate them or the experience to make sense of them. We can provide opportunities to help children play and learn through their storytelling.

It is useful to make a collection of fairy tale toys and small world resources that can be used to prompt the children into creating their stories. Creating a storytelling space in the classroom further validates storytelling. Provide floor space for rolls of paper, drawing space on papered walls and attractive notebooks of all shapes, sizes and colours. A thoughtfully designed cosy area with soft furnishings surrounded by castles, forests and seaweed, even a media player loaded with sound effects can all inspire and transport children to a land where stories will flourish and grow.

Children as tellers of tales

Storytelling is the purest form of philosophical exploration. When we surround our children with the mysteries of human nature, social conventions and the moral and ethical maze that weaves in and out of stories, we are enabling them to think. More importantly, we are introducing a medium that encourages the language of thinking and wondering.

Opening the doors into story worlds enables children to see connections between their own worlds and the stories they tell within them. But it is also important that the stories have not only a context but a consequence too. Stories that are untold cannot be understood, built upon or developed with understanding. The stories that are told in the classroom should be given reference and recognition. Stories are valuable in so many ways: as a tool and vehicle for development and articulation, for the practising of new words and language and of voicing aloud things they see, perceive, dream and fear. Wonderment and worry are dominant themes in the stories our young children tell. When a child recreates conflict, he or she can do so in the mind of a Big Bad Wolf; when he or she needs to work through anger or jealousy, he or she can turn to the safety of the role of somebody else far away in a world where resolution can be achieved. Storytelling has always been the medium through which adults pass on messages to our children, the world is a complex and dangerous place, beware the Big Bad Wolf.

But it is also a world where we want our children to revel in joy and endless possibilities.

When children tell stories to an audience of peers, together they can help bring them to life. The roles are given voices, the voices are given choices and the choices themselves are given a dialogue through enquiry.

Below are some examples of stories my children have asked to have written down for sharing with the class. The stories are influenced on the most part by familiar and well-loved books and fairy tales, but interwoven among the familiar are things that puzzle the audience: strange behaviours and strange happenings in unfamiliar worlds that need clarification and analysis. Through philosophical facilitation, we are able to ask questions that explore the nature of life's mysteries. Why do bad things happen? Why are friends so important? How will we ever know what is real?

Kelsey – The dragon and the witch

There was a big castle and next to it was a big dragon, a really mean dragon and a prince and a princess. There was a forest and the prince and princess were walking through it and they didn't notice a tree had fallen down and there was a witch hiding behind it. The witch made a spell and trapped the princess behind the tree and tied her round it. Then there was a thunderstorm with thunder and the princess was trapped in it then the dragon came back and rescued her and all the magic was gone. Then a king came and turned into a bear that was going to eat the dragon. She ran into her house, ran up the stairs and slammed the door shut and hid under her bed and was crying and crying, and she told her daddy then everyone lived happily ever after.

Shauna – Little Red Riding Hood

Little Red Riding Hood got some flowers and she forgot to give them to her grandma. She wanted to give her some cup of tea. She said, look a big, big, big Queen. Goldilocks wanted her to see her duck but her duck was too busy eating food and she said what do you want to eat? I want some food but what big ears you have and then the crocodile camed and did a big roar. What did you eat for your tea today crocodile?

But he wanted to be friends but he couldn't find any so Goldilocks said to him do you want to eat me? But she quickly got on his back and fell so sleepy she laid back on the crocodile.

Kelsey – Right, this is a story – The witch and all the fairy tales

One day there was a wicked witch and she was a wicked witch and she was nasty. She had a magic wand but she didn't want to do it on Rapunzel. The Queen wanted to keep the fairy tales for herself and she didn't want Rapunzel to keep them.

She said, it's mine forever and ever and she didn't want anyone to spoil her fairy tale ever.

Then one day there was a nice fairy and she spelled the nasty witch and the naughty Queen. Then Rapunzel realised she wanted to keep it for everyone to just keep safe. The end.

Poppy – The princess and the wolf

Once upon a time there was a little girl called Rapunzel and she was walking through the forest and suddenly she looked out of her window and saw a wolf and he was going to blow her house down. All she found was a Wicked Queen who locked her in a tower and every day the Queen bought food for Rapunzel. A monster came every day and Rapunzel got a pen and drawed a line then out of the monster's tummy came a prince and he married Rapunzel and then they lived happily ever after.

Kelsey – This is my story, let me write the story down before I read it to you. It's called 'Do you mind being my friend? Would you be my princess?'

Once upon a time she wanted to be the same but she couldn't be the same so she got a nice Princess Queen. It would be helpful if you wanted to be friends. Friends or being sad? Friends are being very happy. The end.

Kelsey – Lovely shoes and the birthday cake

King's going to come and someone's peeping– I don't know who it is yet.

Good fairy flies and king is going in the castle and Mary Mary has to look for her sheep and she goes walking. Mary Mary needs quickly to find her sheep the storm is coming. Then it gets thunder. Here comes thunder, now rain, rain and dragon is going. He don't like rain. Roar . . .

Unicorn is coming now, hopping on two legs, who is best at hopping? Unicorn or goat or Mary Mary? Where is that witch? Ah, she is going to dance in the rain.

Taylor – The shark and the dragon

The shark and the dragon went hunting for food. They found some and they ate it off the floor. Then he started fighting the dragon and the man ran out and started shouting. Knock knock, can I come in the castle? No I will smack you and break you and have your sister for dinner. Then a wolf came and ate the dragon. Roar, roar he fell down and the house broke, it broke for ever. Then the wolf came back to cut down the castle and out ran the dragon and he ate a horse. Mrs Fork the wicked witch came and she goed in the house and saw a princess. You can stay there and sleep for a hundred years ha ha ha.

Chloe – Little elf

Once upon a time there was an elf. An old elf called Peter and now he's very tiny and lives with a big tiger. He likes not believing his eyes. The tiger is really poorly and needs to get to the doctors so the elf pulled him by the tail out of the house. The end.

Many of these children's stories were shared with the class. Sometimes the children chose friends to help act them out, sometimes they asked for them not to be shared with others but kept secret in the book. Other times we invited parents in to listen to these stories being read and performed. Through sharing these stories parents begin to understand that early education is not about phonics and keywords and reading schemes but a love of story, of the spoken and written word, of the joy of presenting a performance and ownership of a new world. These stories also encourage parents to talk together with their children. What happens next? Why do dragons need friends? Are all stepmothers wicked? The examples above highlight children's preoccupations with issues such as wanting to be friends, needing to gain power and control. They involve making choices, sharing, transformation, resolution, rescue and revenge and most fittingly of all not believing our eyes.

The power of the fairy tale

Fairy tales are a crucial aid to a young child's moral education. It is through immersion in story that empathic understanding begins. How does a little pig deal with being chased by a Big Bad Wolf? What would it feel like to be in possession of magic beans? And why do people do bad things? In fairy tales, the child puts him- or herself in the position of the hero or heroine. He or she finds resolution to worries about loss, separation, uncertainty and conflict. Without fairy tales how is a child to understand what we as humans and as a wider society believe are our moral and ethical obligations.

In my setting, we have a storytelling area near the book corner. Here, the children have access to fairy tale figures, picture cards and other small world story boxes. This is where many stories are created, told, scribed and acted out. The following dialogue took place in this area among a group of three girls. The sorting game was their own invention.

This division of good and bad characters happens frequently as the following examples show.

Case study

Pretend play with the fairy tale characters – 'Goodies and baddies' dialogue

Nell:	Let's put all the lovelies in the castle
Grace:	This girl with a fish is lovely
Jess:	But she is swimming – not in the castle she can be good outside
Facilitator (F):	Did you know some mermaids like this one have very sharp teeth?
Nell:	She not smiling
F:	So is she a goody then?
Grace:	Yes – there is some fairies, they is lovely too
F:	Oh I have found a King, he is wearing lovely clothes isn't he? Can he come in?
Macy:	No, he's not a lovely
Nell:	He is a nasty. He's not a girl
F:	Are only girls lovelies then?
Nell:	Yes
F:	But this pixie you have put here is a boy isn't he?

(I don't think she had realized this)

	Can he still be a lovely?
Macy:	Yes he can can't he Nell?
Nell:	*(thoughtful)* Mmm
F:	So now you have a boy there can the King be a lovely too?
Nell:	No but he can be a lovely over there by himself

This time I noticed a group of boys hovering close by and explained what the girls had been doing. I was interested to see what would happen if they were to sort the baddies. . . .

Baddies – A dialogue with boys

Harry:	This one hungry wolf is 'cos he's got sharp teeth and eats something – a girl
Noah:	And this wicked witch – she is scary and I don't like her
F:	But she looks like quite a nice witch, she is smiling isn't she?
Noah:	No she is doing spells in her head – all witches are bad
F:	What if you were a frog and she did a spell to turn you back into a little boy again? Would she be good then?
Noah:	No she would put me back to a frog and put me in the big oven

Hayden:	This hunchback is bad – his face is bad
F:	Does it matter that he has a bad face? How do we know he is bad?
Hayden:	He will be bad when people come in his castle
Noah:	(*picks up the mermaid*) What is this?
F:	She is a mermaid with sharp teeth which we can't see
Noah:	Then she be bad
Henry:	This monster is bad (*Minotaur*) he is cross
F:	Are you bad when you have a cross face?
Henry:	No, my teeth's not sharp
Billy:	This monster is Sully he is good
F:	But he is a monster, why is he not bad like these other ones?
Billy:	He is smiling so he is a good monster
F:	What if this ogre smiles? Is he good too?
Noah:	No he is bad he's not happy and he has these (sword and axe)
	He's bad 'cos he's not happy
Hayden:	I be bad when someone shouts at me. . .

In this example, we discover that children's impressions of characters are based mainly on appearance. The facilitator's role here was to encourage the children to think about behaviour rather than appearance. In order for children to start to explore philosophical questions about moral and ethical behaviour, they must first learn to recognize these behaviours. Once recognized, these behaviours begin to infiltrate and influence their play, language and thinking.

Using fairy tale puppets

I have highlighted three case studies using the puppets with a group of nursery children. Each case study focuses on the development of the facilitator as a listener and shows how listening provides opportunities for questioning. The third case study shows how this questioning transfers to the children enabling them to take the first steps as facilitators themselves.

These case studies use puppets or representations of fairy tale characters to gauge children's perceptions of stereotypical behaviours. Fairy tale characters are representations of behaviour, representing good and evil, power and powerlessness, wealth and poverty.

> *The following activity encourages children to explore the nature of these behaviours in the context of discovering what makes humans good or bad and most importantly, why?*

Activity: What is a witch?

Resources: A witch puppet, toy or illustration. A thinking card for each child.

Pass around a puppet or picture of a traditional witch. Ask the children to comment about things they notice or already know about the witch. Record their comments on paper and ask the children to decide whether they think she is a good character or a bad character using their thinking card. Start the dialogue by asking children to explain why they voted good or bad.

Case study

Fifteen nursery children with one term's philosophy experience.

Thinking about the witch puppet

Taylor:	He's got a long nose
Jorja:	Actually it has long wormy hair
Madison:	It's got a long hat
Ashley:	Her got a top, it got a star on
Sky:	It got pointy shoes and black
Tilly:	She got green eyes
Olivia:	She got green eyes and grey hair
Ella:	They're naughty so they have green eyes
Kennedy:	Witches do spells
Demi:	Witches have got dancing arms

The children were then asked to show their thinking cards indicating whether they thought the witch was good or bad. These results were recorded and the children were asked to give their reasons for why she might be GOOD.

Demi:	She got a nice face, she's smiling
F:	But is she smiling because she's kind?
	Do you think she smiles when she is doing bad spells?
Kennedy:	Yes she does, she turns people into frogs and laughs, ha ha ha
Tilly:	Yes she's saying something magic and saying ha ha ha
Ella:	She might turn me into a butterfly and that would be good

F:	Do you mean that she would be a good witch if she turned you into a butterfly?
Ella:	Yes
F:	So what would you think if she turned you into a frog?
Dylan:	She would be a mean witch then
F:	But what if you didn't like butterflies?
Henry:	Yes I don't like butterflies but I might like being a frog
Olivia:	She only turns people into nasty things not nice things 'cos that's what witches do
Kennedy:	They only like doing bad stuff to people so they get cross then she laughs like this hahaha
F:	So are you saying that witches enjoy being mean?
Tayla:	Yes that's 'cos they are baddies not goodies
Lucy:	Baddies hate goodies that's why they do nasty things
F:	So when she smiles is the witch a baddie?

Most children indicated agreement with this question.
I asked the children to vote again. Is the witch good or bad? This time, the voting revealed that four out of the original five children had changed their minds from initially thinking she was good to now thinking she was bad.

In these early days of enquiry, the role of the facilitator is to ask questions that offer the children an alternative viewpoint. In the above case study, I wanted to move the children away from the assumption that anyone who smiles might automatically be good. Some members of the group quickly recognized the distinction between a good smile and an evil one and gave examples of witches laughing as they performed evil deeds. This may have helped other members of the group understand the difference between appearance and behaviour.

Case study

Thinking about the Big Bad Wolf puppet

This session involved looking at the character of the Big Bad Wolf. Again, we passed him round the circle and invited children to contribute their thoughts and ideas about him.

Lucy:	He is bad he has sharp teeth
Gemma:	He eats Red Riding Hood
Madison:	He doesn't eat boys only girls
Lucy:	That's because he is a boy
F:	Does anyone else think he only does bad things?
Madison:	He doesn't like children does he?
F:	Are people who don't like children bad do you think?
Lucy:	But the wolf eats good people and bad too
F:	If I had sharp teeth and claws would I be bad too?
Olivia:	No because you are not a wolf
F:	Could I dress up as a grandma and be bad?
Olivia:	No you can't eat children because you are not a wolf

From this short sample of the dialogue, we can identify a growing number of assumptions. Before we push children into detailed philosophical reasoning, it is important for the facilitator to listen to the children's preconceptions. It is through analysis of these that we can develop our own questioning skills.

The following statements best describe the children's ideas about the wolf

- Only boy wolves are bad
- Wolves have no preference whether they eat boys or girls
- Wolves don't like children
- Wolves eat good people and bad people
- People do not behave in the same way as wolves.

As facilitators, we can use these statements and turn them into questions to further develop thinking and reasoning. For example, we might wish to ask one or more of the following questions:

What makes boy wolves behave differently from girl wolves? (Philosophical content of gender)

What makes a wolf different from a person? (Nature of humans and animals)

Does a wolf know the difference between good and bad behaviours? (Moral understanding)

Case study

Activity: Choosing friends for dragon

 Resources: A selection of fairy tale puppets, toys or picture cards
Explain to the children that a dragon finds it very hard to make friends.
Put out a selection of fairy tale characters (puppets or picture cards) and
ask the children to think carefully about which characters might be good
friends for the dragon to have.

This was an early enquiry with 18 nursery children. This was a follow-up
to a previous session where we had explored why the dragon found it hard
to make friends.

F:	Can you remember why dragon didn't find it easy to make friends?
Shauna:	He ran away from his friends
Poppy:	Because he's got sharp teeth
Harry:	And he growled
F:	Did anyone think of any good friends for dragon?
Poppy:	Little red riding hood was his friend
Millie:	Was she nice to the dragon Poppy?
Poppy:	Yes
Henry:	This one did, he bangs down trees and has a smiley face (*points to woodcutter puppet*)

Kelsey:	If he have a smiley mouth he allowed to be friends with the dragon
Harry:	All smiley faces can be friends. They good puppets.
Millie:	This one can't she is an evil witch
Poppy:	No Millie, look, she is a nice witch, she has a smiley mouth
F:	Do you agree or not Millie?
Millie:	Yes I've changed my mind I think. She is nice I think
Ella:	She's got a mean face. She put a spell on him. She couldn't even count when they played hide and seek.
Jude:	Policeman played with dragon
F:	Do you think they played nicely together?
Jude:	Yes 'cos he a policeman – he just has to stop all the cars
	The thing came and chopped him
	He was mean
F:	Does anyone else agree that this policeman is mean?

(Millie and Jessica say yes)

Jude:	He knocked over the tree to get to the policeman. Policemans normally stop people doing homework. My sister tried to do homework and he tried to take her away.
Shauna:	Wolf didn't play nicely with the dragon 'cos he was not good
Kelsey:	He was mean
Millie:	Did he growl?
Kelsey:	Yes he bited him with his teeth.
Catie:	I think the queen was nice to dragon
	'Cos she played hide and seek
Millie:	No she was mean, 'cos her eyebrows are pointing down
F:	*(I pulled a mean face while speaking in nice voice)* I think you are very lovely children. I am a nice queen aren't I?
Millie, Shauna and Kelsey:	[N]o you are not nice

(The rest of the group thought I was being nice)

Kelsey:	Grandma was nice because she cooked him a nice tea.
F:	What do you think about the prince? Was he a good friend or not?
Kelsey:	No he mean he got a stick thing (sword) he hit dragon and hit him
	The stick was mean
F:	So if he didn't have the sword would he have been nice to the dragon?

Millie: Yes he would have run away I think but maybe his mum would say play nicely

Poppy: And the king would say that because he wants people to be friends even with dragons.

The puppets were then photographed in two groups to represent the children's decisions; good friends or not good friends and the puppets were left on the carpet for children to use in their play.

The following is a transcript of a child extending this session through her play. Kelsey, the child in question, was not yet confident enough to share her ideas in the dialogue. However, the following extract shows how she uses play to make sense of what she has heard in the session and her own thoughts about the dragon.

Jessica (wolf) chases Kelsey (dragon) around carpet.

Kelsey: Stop it he's not being nice stop chasing me. I don't like being chased

Dragon is going to be rabbit's friend all day. They are going to bed and everybody going say goodnight and every night if they got smiley mouth they can say goodnight. (*She picks up Red Riding Hood*) she be nice they gonna play dragons

(Millie interrupts the play. She is helping set up the snack cups and bowls nearby)

Millie: I'm going to give myself the pink bowl at snack time

F: Don't you want to give that one to your friend?

Millie: Hmm I might do, well I might give a red cup to Poppy and a yellow one to me

F: Are red cups better?

Millie: Yes, how many red cups are there?

F: Two I think

Millie: Well then I will give a red cup to Poppy and one to me

(Kelsey meanwhile has taken the dragon to the drawing table and returns to show it to me)

Kelsey: I drawed a dragon it got fire

Millie: Why has it got fire?

F: I think I may have seen dragons like this with fire, have you Kelsey?

Kelsey: Yes if dragon roars I won't be his friend

Millie: I will be his friend

Kelsey: If he roars no one will be his friend. (*She looks again at her picture and points to the fire*) you need to rub it out, with a sponge

Millie: Shall I draw a dragon with fire?

Kelsey: Yes but now I'm drawing Red Riding Hood. See I drawed a friend for dragon. I drawn a smiley pirate. He is going to a party

F: Whose party?

Kelsey: Her, remember her? (*Goes to carpet and fetches the princess puppet*)

(*Millie fetches a different dragon that was in the small world area, this one has plastic flames coming out of his mouth*)

Kelsey: That one not allowed to come to the party

F: Why not?

Kelsey: 'Cos he be naughty and he got fire

F: What about the puppet dragon, has he got fire?

Millie: No, he hasn't got fire. He hasn't got an open mouth– he is not roaring

Kelsey: I don't like the other dragon he roaring, he scary.

This extract from Kelsey's play illustrates her conflict between finding a friend for the dragon and the possibility that the dragon might be fierce and frightening. Her thinking remains consistent in that she does not like dragons who 'have fire and roar', yet she obviously feels empathy with the friendly dragon we talked about in the session. Through play, Kelsey is able to work through this conflict.

Fairy tale activities

Activity: Would you rather? – Little Red Riding Hood's basket

Resources: A copy of Little Red Riding Hood four pieces of paper on which should be drawn. One of each mentioned four items.

Read the story together and ask the children to think about the following question.

Next time Little Red Riding Hood meets a wolf, what would she rather have in her basket?

> An information book about wolves?
> A get away vehicle?
> An axe?
> Or a woodcutter?

Ask the children to choose which object they think would benefit her most and stand by that card. Encourage each group to talk together first about why they made that choice. Assemble all children back into a circle and ask them to share their reasons and ideas together. After the dialogue, you may wish to ask them to vote again taking into consideration what has been discussed. Note whether any children have changed their minds and if so why?

Case study

Little Red Riding Hood's basket

A group of 18 nursery children aged 4 years with two term's experience of philosophy.

I read the story of Little Red Riding Hood to the children and asked them to think about choosing some things they could put in her basket to help her next time she met a wolf.

I had originally pre-prepared the abovementioned four items but decided not to share these with the children until they had come up with ideas of their own. I was pleased to discover that most of the above choices were matched or bettered by the children. In the end, I used just the children's ideas. We discussed these choices and I drew pictorial representations for each choice on a piece of A4 paper to use later in the enquiry.

Dialogue

Holly:	I think we should put fruit in the basket and then when you see the wolf then just throw them at the wolf
Poppy:	Or give it to the wolf and while he is eating it she can just walk off
Jude:	But he might come back and say I want more
Holly:	But she will be back at her house
Harry:	We could give her an axe to chop the wolf up
Henry:	We could get a pan to whack him with
Jude:	Or a gun (we grouped these as weapons)
Poppy:	We need a net to trap him but then he will chew it
Holly:	Maybe we can put him in a cage?
Millie:	How about if it had a lock and a key inside it then he would get out
Holly:	But then we could lock it a lot of times
Henry:	Or put a chain round it
Millie:	But what if he gets out?
Holly:	But what if we just make it a really hard metal so he can't get out
Cybele:	Let's put him in the cage and get those metal things and a big magnet and shake and shake it and it's gonna get dead. The wolf will get dead. The cage flies on to the magnet and you shake it around and the wolf would get dead and it would look funny
Harry:	I would smack him with a pan and then put him in the cage
Ryan:	How about you get a car and run over him and then he'd die and then the police wouldn't ever go and get him and he wouldn't be able to get to hospital
F:	Would you use the car any other way?
Ryan:	I would just drive the wolf somewhere else
Cybele:	You could drop him somewhere where there was no cars
Henry:	Or put him in the car and drive him to prison and lock him and he would never come out again
Tyler:	I would squash him with the car or put him in the sewer
Ryan:	If I was in a car I would get out and scare him away
Holly:	I wouldn't! I would lock it
Tyler:	We could blow up the wheels and get bigger wheels to squash him
Poppy:	I would just drive away really fast

(At this stage I added the information book about wolves)

F:	Is this a story book about wolves?
Several children:	No

I explained that it would tell me all about wolves

Ryan: But I have a question. How would you get a real car in the basket?

F: I think it might have to be a special magic shrinking/growing car

I then explained that they could make only one choice about what Red Riding Hood would have in her basket. I spread the pictures of their chosen objects around the room and asked them to move to the card of their choice. The children were then given talking time in their groups.

We returned to the circle and the children gave their reasons for their choices

At this point, one child said she could not decide, so she had gone with her friend because he likes cars. I asked her to try and explain why she could not make her own choice

F: So do any of these cards match with your thinking?

Jessica: No I don't think so. I need a man to help me, not a wood cutter, not with an axe. A grown up that would help me run. Or a sign that said wolf this way, Red Riding Hood that way. Or maybe I want to lock him up but not in a cage so I'm not sure.

I offered her the chance to listen to other people's reasons and see if it would help her make a choice on the cards available

F: So would anyone like to explain why they chose the axe?

Tyler: I chose the axe because I don't like him

F: Is that ok to kill him just because you don't like him?

Cybele: Yes we can kill baddies

Millie: Not really 'cos baddies don't exist

Poppy: Only animals that are baddies do exist

Kelsey: There are goodie animals like elephants and lambs and butterflies

Harry: A baddie animal does exist, he lives at the zoo

Holly: Like a crocodile that bites or a snake

Cybele: Do you know that vampires bite you? They're not real but if they bite you then you turn into a vampire too

F: Are vampires people or animals?

Cybele: Some people do think they are real people and some think they are animals

F: If you killed a baddie animal would you kill a baddie person?

Cybele:	No, because I like people but I'm not that keen on animals
F:	Who else chose the axe and why?
Harry:	I was going to chop him too
Poppy:	I wouldn't chop him up. I chose the book
F:	Why did you chose the book?
Poppy:	I'm going to read it, it will help me smack his bottom
Catie:	What if we made a book that told us things
Holly:	We will have to think what wolves do, but how do we know about wolves?
Millie:	Our mummies will have to tell us
F:	Did anyone choose the huntsman?
Ryan:	I did. So he could chop him up.
F:	What will he do that you can't do though? Can't you chop him yourself?
Ryan:	The wolf might get a gun and the axe and run away then we will have to run away
F:	Do you always need a grown up to help you?
Several children replied:	Yes
Millie:	Not always, not when there aren't wolves
Holly:	I chose the cage so he couldn't get out
F:	How would you get him in there?
Holly:	It would be hard if you only had a small door not a big one
Poppy:	But what if he didn't want to go in there?
Cybele:	Maybe a piece of wood would push him in
Tyler:	Or maybe a wall would be able to push him in
Cybele:	Then just put a locker and lock it with a key
Millie:	But what if you don't have wood? What if you don't have a key? What if someone who you don't know who it is takes the key?
Poppy:	What about if you just say hello come in my cage and then when he comes near then push him in?
Tyler:	You could push him in a house then push the house in the cage
F:	Why did people choose the car?
Ryan:	When I saw the wolf I would just get in and lock the doors and drive away
F:	Jessica, has that helped you make a choice now? Which one will you choose?

Jessica: I would throw the fruit on him then run away
F: Why did the other people in the group choose fruit?
Shauna: I chose the fruit because I like it
F: How does liking fruit help you?
Shauna: Well I will throw it at him
Henry: You could just peel the banana and throw the skin at his head

This dialogue shows a determination by the group to help each other work out how their choices might work. It provides evidence of an emerging sense of community. The children offer both questions and possible solutions. When Jessica found it hard to make a choice, she could explain why and was able to think again about making a choice by the end, formulating a reason why her choice might work. They understand that it is not important to find a correct answer but collectively work through the pros and cons of their ideas using problem solving as a tool for examining early philosophical concepts, such as power and knowledge.

Activity: Jack and the Beanstalk treasure snatch

Objectives: Ask and answer questions, make relevant contributions, offer suggestions and take turns, work effectively in groups by ensuring that each group member takes a turn challenging, supporting and moving on

 Resources: A copy of the Jack and the Beanstalk handout cut into eight cards.

- Sack of gold
- Photo of Jack's dad that has been stolen from Jack's family
- Magic harp
- Giant cake
- The old woman
- The gardening book
- A skipping rope or length of string

What to do:

Read the story of Jack and the Beanstalk. Ask the children what they think their most valuable possession is and why? Now look together at the six pictures on the handout and discuss what they can see.

Explain that Jack has only got a very short time to escape down the beanstalk with his six treasures before the Giant wakes up. He can only carry one object at a time. The children should help Jack choose which items he should take in which order and why.

Spread the skipping rope along the floor like a beanstalk. Place the 'most important' label from the handout at the bottom and the 'least important' label at the top.

Ask for a volunteer to place an item somewhere on the beanstalk.

Repeat until all six objects are on the line.

Now ask the children whether there are any items they think should be moved and why.

Encourage the children to discuss which items should be moved. Ask questions such as what does this item represent? Is that more or less important than. . .? Why?

Can the children come to a definite order of importance? If not, why not? Which objects caused the most problems in the decision-making process and why?

Activity: Beanstalk lands

This activity will encourage pupils to use their imaginations and philosophical reasoning to choose a land where there can only be one rule. They must decide which land has the best rule to benefit its citizens.

Resources: A copy of Jack and the Beanstalk. *Four beans – four sheets of A4 paper. Write one of the following statements on each sheet.*

a) The land where . . . anyone can declare themselves king or queen at anytime
b) The land where . . . everyone is given an age and stays this age forever
c) The land where . . . all animals are given the same rights as humans
d) The land where . . . nobody has the right to own anything.

What to do:

Explain that Jack has planted four beans and each has grown a separate beanstalk. Jack knows only the name of the land but has not actually been allowed to look above the cloud. The children must help him make a decision about which land to enter.

Spread the four cards into separate spaces and ask the children to move to the card of their choice. Encourage each group to share their reasons with others in their group. Reform the circle and ask each group to present its ideas. Older children may wish to assign a scribe to list all their ideas.

Encourage reasoned discussion about positive and negative aspects of the lands. When all lands have been discussed, allow the children to change their minds and move to a different land if they wish. Ensure that reasons are given for moving.

Activity: Fairy tale corners

The following activity will develop the skill of using the language of philosophical enquiry. Children should be encouraged to make their own choices and justify these choices. Allowing group rehearsal time is beneficial for those not yet confident to make their own choices or voice their ideas in the large group

Resources: Laminate three A4 cards. One card should read 'I agree', one should read 'I disagree' and the third 'I've changed my mind because'; you will also need a list of the fairy tale statements to read out one at a time.

What to do:

Ask the children to stand in the middle of the space. Read out one of the statements from the list below and ask the children to move to the card that best fits their thinking. Allow a few minutes for them to talk together in a group telling at least one person why they moved to that card. Encourage every person in the small group to share his or her voice with someone. Bring the group back to a circle sitting in their divided groups. Allow time to enquire why people agree or disagree with the statements. Repeat using as many statements as you wish. At the end of each dialogue, ask the children if anyone would like to change their minds moving across the 'I've changed my mind' card. Encourage them to say which statements or ideas have influenced their thinking.

Statements:

- It was OK for Goldilocks to eat up baby bear's porridge.
- The princess did not have to keep her promise to a frog.
- Cinderella should have stood up to her sisters.
- Peter Pan should leave Neverland and grow up.
- The three little pigs' mother should not have made them leave home.

- The prince should always marry the prettiest girl.
- Witches should punish people who are not kind.
- The wolf should have been friendly to the pigs.
- It was wrong for Jack to take the giant's gold.
- Jack was foolish to swap his cow for five beans.

In the early stages of practising philosophy with children, it is important to give the children as much exposure to fairy tales as possible. These tales will introduce and develop the skills of empathy, making choices and justifying ideas within a familiar format. The following case study illustrates the thinking that knowledge and understanding of fairy tales encompass and the connections the children make to a wealth of philosophical concepts.

Case study

Fairy tale enquiry, Key Stage 1 – 15 children aged 5, 6 and 7 years
Dialogue – Jack and the Beanstalk
We read the story together and the children were given some quiet reflection time to think about the concepts contained in the story.
The children decided upon the following concepts:

Choice – He had to choose how to stay safe.

Hate – There was hate in the story because the woman and the goose hated the giant and the giant hated everyone because nobody was as big as him.

Rescue – Because the lady and the goose were rescued from the giant.

Trickery – Yes, Jack tricked the giant by hiding.

No that's not tricking, that's just hiding. I think that's **survival**.

Or **protection** from the giant he was protecting himself from being eaten.

I think there was **responsibility** because he was responsible for the three things to get money. He was responsible to get money for his mum but he just got beans so that wasn't responsible if his mum starved.

Fear – Jack and the old woman were scared of the Giant.

Bravery – Because Jack went into the castle by himself.

He was very brave for taking things as well.

I think it's to do with **work** too, that's kind of the same as responsibility, because the old woman had to work for the giant and Jack had to do work for his mum.

I think there was **Love** – *(several children voiced their disagreement)*

Madison defended her choice – I think there was. He loved Daisy and didn't want to sell her.

(The children decided that this was justifiable and so the concept stood)

Curiosity – He wanted to find out about the lair. He wanted to know what was in there so he was curious.

It wasn't a lair it was a castle.

It was like a lair because there was a giant waiting inside.

He wanted to see what the land above the beanstalk was like too.

Punishment – Jack punished the giant by flinging him into space.

And mum throws Jack into bed when he comes home with only beans.

Cleverness – Because Jack had a plan.

So we can have **wisdom** too

Unfair – Why would the giant keep all his money to himself when he should share and all those poor people out there had none? He had lots and lots.

Theft – Jack stole things, the goose, harp and the money.

And he never gave them back, he just stole them.

But the giant was a meanie.

Like a bully.

F: Are there any other concepts that we think we might use to help us with our questioning?

I think **knowledge** because Jack thought of a plan.

The children then drew a picture in their journals and compiled questions based on the concepts that they had chosen. They were asked to say which concept went with their question and to say why.

The following questions were offered by the children

Why did Jack pull down the beanstalk and destroy the giant? (Knowledge, survival).

Why did jack go up the beanstalk? (Theft, curiosity, bravery).

Why did jack think he could survive the giant? (Survival).

Why did the lady work for the giant even though she didn't like him?
(Hate, fear).

Why didn't he sell daisy to get money instead of going up the
beanstalk?

Henry:	Why did he swap her for beans then?
Abbie:	He thought they were magic and that would make him rich
Lavelle:	Maybe he thought the money would grow on trees or bushes?
Henry:	Why didn't he go to the bank then?
Lavelle:	Probably they didn't have banks invented in them days
F:	Ok, what would you rather have magic beans or money?
	The group voted. Only one person chose the beans
Abbie:	I chose magic beans because I could go on adventures instead
F:	Did Jack think there was money at the top of the beanstalk?
Henry:	Yes he was probably thinking there was a world of humans
Olivia:	But it could have been dangerous and the only people who lived there were giants
F:	Would you have gone up if you didn't know there was a giant there?

(Most say yes in response)

Henry:	You can choose to avoid danger by destruction or running away. I would learn skills to survive. But I wouldn't go because the beanstalk looks wobbly, I would think about the danger of falling, that would kill you, falling that far.
George:	We could do a quick check and then run if we see anything bad is going to happen
Madison:	I watch Scooby doo so I'd be prepared for any danger
Tilly:	I wouldn't go up in case there was a giant or a monster
Olivia:	What if I couldn't get down?
Henry:	Well you could get down because you could go down the beanstalk
George:	But what if the old lady or the giant has cut it down then you'd be stranded there
Abbie:	Then I would have to work for the giant or maybe . . . I think I've changed my mind, I'm not going if there is a giant.
Lavelle:	If there was a laser shooting monster then maybe I wouldn't go
Henry:	Yes that would be stupid
Abbie:	But Lavelle, you don't know, that's the thing

Madison: I might take the risk it would be my choice and I would be happy and feel brave if there weren't any laser shooting monsters or maybe they were just tiny and the lasers were like not painful then I would be proud of my choice for being brave.

F: Is it scarier to go if you know what's there or NOT know what's there?

Lavelle: I agree with Madison, I think we should just take a bit of a risk

Abbie: But some people are brave enough like when you're little you've never been on scary rides at the fair and going to school. They say 'I can do it I can do it' and some people don't want to do new things that's why they sometimes cry.

Lavelle: Do you mean like when I started school I cried because I didn't know what was going to happen and I didn't know stuff?

Henry: I think anything new might be scary to some people

George: Not me

F: What makes some people braver than others then?

Henry: Trust and bravery

F: Trust makes people brave? What does that mean?

Abbie: Trust means believing in yourself.

Henry: Yes, trust your choices

Lavelle: Or if someone tells you that you can do it you could trust them

George: If you haven't done it you don't know but I might listen to someone who has done it
I might have a try if my friend told me it was fine but not if someone I didn't know

Following the discussion that had arisen from the questioning section, we returned to collecting the final questions. The next question was:

Why did Jack pull the beanstalk and whoosh the giant away?

Abbie: I think the concept that went with that was knowledge, because he had a plan about what would happen

Olivia: I think it's about hate because Jack hated the giant
He said you've been bad enough this time, this is what you deserve

Henry: I think it was about wisdom
Jack knew that if he didn't ping the giant he would be eaten

George: That was survival as well then

The last question was:

Why did the old lady work for the giant even though she hated him?

Abbie:	She did it because she was scared of him, he kept thundering
Olivia:	She was trying to survive because if she refused the giant would gobble her up
Henry:	She was scared because when you are scared you don't want to do it but you'd be worried about being punished
Abbie:	Well that's about having no choice as well then isn't it Henry?
Henry:	Yes I think being scared does takes away your choice
Abbie:	I think nearly all these questions are about choice aren't they?
Tilly:	Jack did lots of choosing
George:	Or maybe he was just lucky?
Lavelle:	Yes, to get all that gold and the harp and stuff
F:	How was that luck?
Lavelle:	Well the giant might have been not rich in the first place
Henry:	But if he didn't choose in the first place then he wouldn't have been lucky

We had unfortunately reached the end of the session at this point; so I allowed the children to vote on a question to explore further at home. The question they voted for was:

Why did Jack steal?

This case study highlights how familiar the group is at this stage with its ability to connect themes of the book to philosophical ideas. Their questions were connected to concepts and their willingness to ensure that clarification was given for the connections was apparent.

Reflecting on the nature of our children's stories

- How can we find ways to understand children's stories?
- What subjects do your children use in their stories and why?
- How can we find ways of allowing the children to explore the things they talk about?
- What would a world without story be like?
- Would you rather live in a world without story or a world without facts?

3
Big Thinking, Big Ideas: The Role of the Facilitator

This chapter will explore ways that we can move forward in our own thinking as facilitators in order to scaffold and support our children in the acquisition of this skill. In order to add rigour to philosophical thinking, we need to have an understanding of how to make sense of the ideas and questions in light of what they mean philosophically. Without this rigour, enquiry is merely conversation. Understanding philosophical concepts helps us gain the confidence to ask the next big question.

In its simplest form, philosophical rigour might take the form of this three-step process:

1. Present your question about an idea, for example, 'what is love?'
2. Come up with definitions of that idea, for example, 'love is a two way thing . . .'
3. Turn those definitions into questions that can be explored through dialogue. For example, 'is it possible to love and not be loved In return?'

Exploring concepts: The philosophy of life

As a facilitator in the community of enquiry, it is essential to have some interest, knowledge and understanding of philosophical concepts. A skilled facilitator will endeavour to highlight the philosophical elements of the children's statements or questions and help them expand their thinking into that area. Better facilitation means that you must challenge statements and turn them into a question. By challenging what someone says, you endeavour to make them question what they really think and why they think it.

Philosophical thoughts

- Does life have a purpose?
- Should people be punished?
- Did we exist before we were born?
- Can there be a most beautiful thing?
- What is intelligence?
- Will I still be the same person when I am old?
- What makes something true?
- Is the brain different from the mind?
- How do we know something is real?
- Is there such a thing as justice?
- Do we ever have free choice?
- How can you see when your eyes are closed?
- What is the difference between a dream and life?
- What makes you, you?
- Should you always do as you are told?
- Do we feel colour?
- What is true happiness?
- Is it ever right to kill anything?
- How do we know what is right or wrong?
- Where do emotions come from?
- What is the difference between man and beast?

These questions come from examination of statements, assumptions or observations that surround us in our everyday lives. This chapter will explore how we can encourage our children to create their own questions and formulate their own answers based on these important philosophical issues.

What are these big issues?

- Famine/plenty
- Greed/selflessness
- Love/hate
- Wisdom/ignorance
- True/false
- Imaginary/real
- Beauty/ugliness
- Power/impotence
- Rich/poor
- Bravery/cowardly
- Kind/cruel
- Responsibility/careless

Exploring philosophical concepts presents different challenges. Certainly for young children, it is likely to be the first time they have been invited to explain opinions or ideas publicly. In an enquiry, they are told that there may be no one answer but they will be held responsible for our thinking and will be asked to back up our statements with reasoned argument. Therefore, in a philosophical enquiry, we open ourselves to scrutiny; our ideas may be challenged by others. This challenge may be quite unsettling for both students and facilitators. However, philosophy can also be incredibly liberating. The very things that make it unsettling can also be liberating. There is a freedom from the constraints of the expected answer. You can change your mind or be the devil's advocate in order to move your thinking forward. You do not know the route of the argument and neither do you know the destination.

The more we question life the more we begin to philosophize. At some point, we may become so intrigued that we may want to research famous philosophical arguments but my belief is that this is not necessary to become a good philosopher. P4C encourages our children to listen to their own voices and those of their peers in a safe environment where trusting relationships are developed and where they can take risks and make mistakes as they explore their ideas.

Before we can expect children to enter this contract, it is important that we as adults learn to listen to our own voices. Through questioning our own assumptions and opinions, we can become aware of what philosophical concepts or big issues mean to us. It is not our job in an enquiry to share these opinions with the children but to use the questions we ask ourselves to develop the thinking of the group.

The following short scenarios are intended to be an introduction to you as a facilitator. They are examples of some issues that may arise in philosophical enquiries with the children. As a facilitator, it is important that you think about these issues for yourself. This will heighten your awareness of possible philosophical arguments that may arise.

Read these short scenarios and ask yourself, friends, family or colleagues what you think. What further questions do you need to ask to gain deeper understanding of what these important concepts mean to us? Note whether they mean the same to everyone. Would they mean the same to others in the wider world? Do these concepts differ in different cultures or under different circumstances?

These scenarios have been designed to stimulate your thought processes based on your beliefs, experiences or opinions about what these concepts might mean.

What is love?

Carly has a best friend that she has grown up with and loves more than anything in the world. One day, this friend announces that she will be leaving to live on the other side of the world forever. Carly is heartbroken but is able to visit a shop where human beings can be replicated exactly, down to the smallest memory. On the day her friend leaves, Carly has the replica delivered. Does Carly need to miss her friend?

What is love?

Truth

Three explorers visit an unexplored island. Unfortunately, their photographic equipment is lost in the journey. When they return to civilization, they tell of an undiscovered creature. When asked to describe it, all three give differing descriptions and draw similar but different images of it. How do we know what the creature really looked like and whether it really existed?

What is truth?

Wisdom

A pod of aliens come to earth and explain that they need the ten wisest men from each planet to help save the universe. They demand that the people choose these candidates. How should the population decide whom to send?

What is wisdom?

Beauty

A world famous artist puts on an exhibition to display what he believes is his finest work and is, in fact, the most beautiful painting ever created. Every person who views this painting hates it. Can it be called the most beautiful painting?

What is beauty?

Free will

You discover that all human beings' actions and thoughts are being controlled by a giant thought machine computer. You are the only person who knows this. Everybody else is acting, thinking and speaking as they are programmed to. Does the fact that you know this computer exists mean that everybody else has no free will?

What is free will?

Identity

Twin boys are born identical in every way. They are separated within an hour and one is transported to the other side of the world from his twin. As they grow up, they look the same, behave the same, have the same likes and dislikes and wear the same clothes. What is it that gives them separate identities?

What is identity?

These scenarios are not for use with children but to develop your, the facilitator's, thinking. To further develop experience in your facilitation, we can use the very books that we will later use with our children.

These books contain a wealth of themes and philosophical ideas that we need to explore. Using the very best of our picture books for children provides the vital link between the children's earlier experiences of playing with and telling stories and the ability to abstract their thinking in a more multilayered way. Using, sharing and valuing children's own stories will give them an understanding of philosophical grammar. We will expect them to bring this to their analysis of picture books further down the line. Understanding how multifaceted picture books work is something many adults may not have had the opportunity to do during their education; so it is equally valid for us to revisit or familiarize ourselves with this skill. If we as adults do not fully understand how to make sense of these books philosophically, then we cannot expect our children to either.

Using the following favourite P4C texts referenced in Chapter 8 on page 162, the hidden world inside the picture book, we can explore a wide range of concepts, for example:

- In *Duck, Death and the Tulip*, we can explore, death, friendship, fear, loyalty, trust, love, knowledge, fate
- In *Burglar Bill*, theft, choice, family, need, remorse, duty, morality
- In *Little Red Hood*, trickery, revenge, survival, courage, cruelty, appearance, murder
- In *Leon and the Place Between*, magic, reality, truth, wisdom, identity, discovery
- In *Where the Wild Things Are*, dreaming, imagination, power, leadership, responsibility, punishment
- In *Denver*, subterfuge, wealth, happiness, equality, free will, envy, hate, democracy
- In *Tadpole's Promise*, identity, transformation, love, wish fulfilment, nature, honesty

The aforementioned are a sample of common concepts that could arise in philosophy sessions with children, and the books listed are very powerful texts to work with.

In my experience, I have found that taking the time to explore concepts contained in picture books with practitioners has developed their understanding and knowledge of philosophical themes prior to working in this way with the children.

The activity below is useful for staff to share at a staff meeting to aid facilitation or can be used with more experienced children to develop deeper questioning skills and conceptual understanding.

Activity: What's in a book?

Method: Choose a selection of picture books or other interesting stimuli. Ask participants to list as many concepts as they think apply to the chosen book/stimuli; for example, this book is about wealth, friendship, power etc.

Decide which concepts you would like to explore further. On a large sheet of paper, write the title 'what is . . .' and add the concept that has been chosen, one per sheet. In groups, list as many statements, assumptions, observations or sayings that you feel sum up this concept.

For example:

What is wealth?

Ask members of the group to offer statements that they think sum up the question, for example:

- Wealth is a way to be happy
- Wealth is not just money
- Money makes the world go round
- Without wealth, you are poor
- The rich get richer the poor get poorer
- Money gives you power.

Allow a few minutes for this part of the activity. Ask the participants to swap their large sheets of paper with another group. Now challenge each group to read through the list of statements they have been given. It is worth noting that they know nothing about where these statements have come from in terms of context, in the same way that statements, assumptions or observations are thrown into a philosophical enquiry.

After reading through these statements, participants should choose some of the statements and turn them into questions, for example, money gives you power might become does money equal power?

The process of turning these statements into questions should provoke dialogue and debate about interpretation of statements and which questions it might lead to.

Introducing concepts to the children

When working with younger children, I introduce the concepts through puppets and fairy tale characters first and then move on to books and other stimuli.

In the early enquiries with young children, we introduce the concepts by overtly saying, 'when you talk about people wanting something they don't have, that is called jealousy.'

We have provided a bank of concept cards at the back of this book and on the companion website that you can photocopy or download, laminate and use to introduce your children to these concepts as they arise.

The following is an extract from an enquiry where we worked together on understanding concepts. This case study illustrates how a group of more experienced children were able to use the cards as visual reminders. Having the cards in front of them helped them to identify the main issues in the book and focused their questioning on these issues. This procedure automatically created more purposeful and philosophical questions.

Case study

Philosophy club

Castles by Colin Thompson – Using the illustration on the page titled Noah's ark

I allowed time for the children to share and discuss what they could see in the picture. I then read the caption 'Most people don't know that Noah had a sister ...'

I then asked the children, tell me what they knew of the traditional Noah's ark story.

The children then drew their own Norah's ark and composed a question about the stimulus.

It was explained that the children would be matching the concept cards with their questions.

I spread out the concept cards and asked the children to find the card that best matched their question, or maybe more than one.

Facilitator (F):	Which concepts are in the story?
Henry:	Hate – Noah hated his sister because she had a better ark
George:	I think he was a bit jealous
Abbie:	Are you saying he hated his sister?

Abbie: (cont.) Because I don't think he did. He wouldn't hate his sister. No he didn't hate, you can't hate a sister. He was just jealous of her

F: Are they 2 separate concepts then?

Abbie: Yes, Norah didn't mean to do it better than him, well she might have done it because she thought nobody respected her or she might not have done it because she didn't want to upset him

F: What does respect mean, Abbie?

Abbie: Well it means that nobody thinks she can do it well and so they laugh at her or don't take her seriously.

F: Is there anything about **freedom**? *(Holds up **freedom** card)*

Lavelle: Yes, Noah escaped with his family and the animals escaped the flood so they were free, they wanted to free the animals even though some animals didn't survive only the ones that can swim

George: I think power, because the woodworms were powerful to get through the wood

Freya: Norah had power. She managed to build that ark really well and managed to balance the towers on it too.

Henry: It could mean intelligent as well

F: What does intelligent mean?

Henry: Think really well

George: You mean write a plan?

Henry: Yes if you copy a plan really well that's intelligent *(F holds up **rules** card)*

George: The rules on Norah's ship were not to sink the ship and the woodworms broke the rules

F: Can animals break rules?

George: Well I think they must have rules because they all do the same sort of things. Like zebras all just graze and lions all attack you don't have attacking zebras that would be breaking the rules.

F: But who decides the rules? Do rules have to be verbally agreed on?

Henry: I don't think they have to be because animals don't talk

Olivia: But they might communicate with snorting or roaring?

F: I think there was **anger** *(Abbie picks up the **anger** card from the floor)*

Abbie: There was a little bit because they got cross with each other

Madison: Well I don't think she got the chance to be cross because she died before she knew he put the woodworms in her ark

*(George identifies the **punishment** card)*

That means when Noah was cross with Norah so he punished her
'Cos he broke something

*(Tilly picks the **wealth** card)*

Yes, he had that ark

Olivia: But he wasn't rich he didn't buy it, he made it

F: So can we include this card then? Can anyone give a justification for having this concept?

(The group disagrees with Tilly and she is happy to discard it)
*(Lavelle picks the **trickery** card up with some uncertainty)*

Abbie: Yes, Noah tricked Norah. He said before they set off: Norah I will not put woodworms in your boat:
He shouted; your boat will not sink

Henry: But that's not a trick, that's a lie

F: Are lies the same as tricks?

Abbie: No tricks are not as bad as lies

F: Is your statement about trickery or lying then?

Henry: I think actually it is about being smart
Noah was smart
He had the great idea of putting the woodworms on the ship

Abbie: But Norah built the best ship

Lavelle: He just did what he was told to do

Henry: I think Norah is the smartest now

Lavelle: I've changed my mind. I think her too, she did build a big ark by herself

George: I disagree, Noah was cleverest because he tamed the woodworm not to eat his boat but trained them to eat her boat when he knew the flood was coming

Henry: Maybe he knew. But he wasn't the cleverest because he only knew the woodworm were able to eat boats because someone told him that

F:	So if someone tells you something does that mean you are not clever?
Tilly:	No it doesn't mean you are clever it means someone else is clever
F:	So if I told you the world was round and you hadn't known that and then you tell someone else who didn't know that, would you be clever or the person who told you be clever?
Abbie:	The person who told you . . . but what if someone had told him? Or someone had told him and so on and so on
F:	And so if the person you told tells someone else, who is the cleverest then? You or the person you told?
Henry:	You
Abbie:	. . . oh, I think I'm a bit muddled now It's the person who started telling the news that's the cleverest isn't it?
F:	So how do you get to be clever?
Lavelle:	We learn stuff
Henry:	But that's people telling us things so is it us or our teachers?
Abbie:	Well we are clever too because we remembered what the teachers said and then we can be clever to tell someone else.
Henry:	But maybe people don't know that someone has already said it before so they think they are the first person to say it so if it comes from their brain they must be clever
Abbie:	Someone has to think of it first, maybe we know things without someone telling us? Like Noah knew wood worms ate wood instead of were made out of wood?
George:	Yes I agree, He just knew they would eat the boat out of his own idea of what wood worm means.
F:	What about **responsibility**? *(I held up the **responsibility** card)*
Olivia:	Yes, she was looking after the animals and so was Noah
Abbie:	But he wasn't caring about his sister and she should be more important than the animals He was only caring about his animals not the ones on Norah's boat
George:	He was only half responsible
F:	Is it better to be responsible for only some animals than no animals or should he have been responsible for all the animals?
Abbie:	Well it's not responsible to only save some At first I think he was caring more for his sister and tried to save her but then when he got jealous it changed him and he stopped caring about her as much because he was jealous maybe he didn't mean her to sink

F:	OK, We have got lots of concepts to work with now. Now we have thought about the concepts we might be able to make the questions more philosophical
Abbie:	I think we should ask 'why didn't Noah care as much about his sister as he did before she built her own ark. Why did he change?'
Henry:	I want to ask 'why did he sink the boat when he didn't need to do such a bad thing?'
Olivia:	Did Noah care more about the animals more than his sister?
George:	I want to ask 'who was cleverest out of Noah and Norah?'

Summary: The group was confident identifying and justifying which concepts they felt were contained in the stimulus. The choosing of the concepts provoked initial dialogue which was a starting point for further exploration in the enquiry, both in this session and the follow-up talk they shared with parents as homework. Taking time to identify these concepts also produced better questioning based on the analysis of the group's understanding of what each concept meant in the context of the stimulus.

Better questioning

When children understand what concepts they are dealing with, they can ask more philosophical questions. They are no longer asking questions for the sake of asking questions but presenting a way to move forward in a topic they are genuinely interested in pursuing. The following case study shows how I first introduce questioning skills to a group of nursery children.

Case study

Children asking questions – Using the book Why Do Stars Come Out at Night?

A stimulus used with 20 nursery children. We read the book together. The story involves a small girl asking her grandfather several questions about the things they see on their walk. Grandad gives humorous answers. We read his answers and offered some answers of our own too. I then asked the children whether we could ask grandad some more questions:

How do fairies get their magic wands?

Ella

How do princesses get their tiaras?

Kennedy

Why are some princesses angry?

Yasmin

F:	What is a question?
Holly:	It means someone wants to talk to you
Cybele:	You have to give a question mark
Poppy:	And give the answer
F:	Do we always find an answer?
Holly:	We do sometimes but if we go in one country we do and some countries we don't
Millie:	You don't get an answer in another country because we can't get the same languages and we don't understand
Poppy:	And if we don't have an answer in our head we can't answer them
F:	Let's try a few questions to see if we can get answers
F:	How did you get to school today?
Lexie:	In the car
F:	How do we know that?
Ryan:	Because I saw(ed) her
F:	So we know that is true because we saw her in her car? Did I get a good answer then?
Ryan:	Yes [b]ut if there was so many cars how would we know which one was Lexies?
F:	Do we need to ask another question then?
Jessica:	We could ask her what colour her car is?
Holly:	There are so many colours in the rainbow and how would we know if she hadn't told us which colour hers was?
Ryan:	If they were so many colours and the same colours how would we know which was Lexies?
Tyler:	We could ask her what shape it is? If it's flat or goes over?
F:	Sometimes we can find the answer out by asking more questions. Sometimes we don't get one answer we get lots but we don't always know which ones we think.

F:	Do you remember some of the questions in this book? Do you think we found any answers to those questions?
Poppy:	Some we did
	We didn't answer 'why is the grass green?'
Cybele:	Yes we did. . . because it is
Catie:	Some children thinked it was purple and some thinked it was green and some people thought it depended what colour your skin is
F:	That was a puzzling idea wasn't it?
Millie:	But if it was in the book we could easily get an answer from Grandad
F:	Shall we think of some more questions to ask Grandad? Is he good at answering questions?
Millie:	Yes [b]ut what if Grandad hasn't got an answer?
Tyler:	So we can ask someone else
Jessica:	We can ask the mermaids
Poppy:	But how do we know what the answer is?
F:	I think maybe we could help each other find some answers by talking and listening together
	Shall we draw our own grandad and ask him some questions like in the book?
Cybele:	No because how can he listen? He hasn't got any ears?
Harry:	Well we can draw him some ears
Poppy:	But how can he still listen because he's only a picture.
F:	We will have to pretend today I think. There, he's finished
Children:	Hello Grandad
F:	Has anybody got a question for Grandad?
Catie:	Why do you need to have hands?
Jude:	Why do some mans have glasses?
Holly:	Why is the sky blue and why is the sea blue?
Kelsey:	Why everything is white?
Poppy:	Not everything is white (children point out different colours)
F:	Can we change that question then?
Kelsey:	Yes why is everything different colours? And why do we have white?
Jude:	It's not a rainbow colour
F:	Is this (blue) thing white?
Children:	No
F:	What if I told a baby this was white? Would he think it was white? What if I call it white?
Millie:	No he would look at it and say it's blue
Poppy:	But how can he talk?

F:	How do babies know what colour things are?
Cybele:	They know and they nod their head
F:	Do they know without anyone telling them?
Millie:	If he points to something then you know what he wants
F:	Do they know everything when they are born?
Children:	No
Millie:	I think their mummy just tells them everything
F:	Maybe another day we can think about knowing things, that's called knowledge in philosophy.
F:	Has anyone else got a question for grandad?
Ryan:	Why is our skin so white?
Tyler:	It isn't, its pink
Jessica:	Why is Cybele's so dark?
Catie:	Hers is different it is brown and ours isn't
Cybele:	That's why my mummy and sister have same as my colour skin

(We have discussed differences and ethnicity on several occasions previously)

Kyle:	Why does Kieran have an implant?
Harry:	'Cos when he was born he can't hear
Ryan:	That's why he be born and his ears don't work very well
Jude:	He can hear us but not if he didn't have it on
F:	I think granddad will have fun thinking about these questions
F:	I'm going to read out your questions and you can help think what these questions are asking about? There are 2 sorts of questions here. I will read them out to you.

(I read the questions to do with people)

Poppy:	We are asking questions about people.
F:	Do you think all people are the same?
Millie:	No, Cybele isn't white. She isn't the same colour
F:	And Kieran has an implant and some are small. Some of us are big and have blond hair.
Holly:	You're still old but you're still small
Ella:	Shauna is 4 but that means she's still small
Poppy:	Old people are already 4 but Eva, Tyler, Kyle, Naiara are new and they're still 3 so they're still small
Millie:	The new people are small
F:	So instead of asking Grandad lots of different questions could we ask him just one about people?
Ella:	We are all different
Kelsey:	Yes we can tell why are we all different?

Shauna:	I'm not small
	I'm nearly getting bigger
Holly:	You are still old but you are still small
Poppy:	She's 4 but she's still small
F:	The other questions were all about something else weren't they?
Harry:	They were about colour things
F:	We could ask 'what is a colour?' Or why do we have coloured things or maybe it's a different question about colours?
Millie:	Like do babies know about colours?
F:	That would be a very interesting question to ask wouldn't it?

Summary

In the early days of enquiry, children still have a tendency to confuse statements with questions. Modelling how we can turn statements into questions is often a necessary technique. Children need to be taught that a question requires some sort of response. In this case study, the children made connections between the experience of answering questions in the book and the questions they wanted to ask. At this stage, we were not aiming for the questions to be philosophical; however, my facilitation did highlight interesting questions conveying the message to the children that these are the questions we value.

Case study

This session with more experienced children aims to illustrate the potential for developing questioning skills. As the quality of questioning improves, so do the level of dialogue and philosophical content.

Philosophy club – 'Asking better questions' session

F:	Today we are going to be thinking about philosophical questions. I've got one for you to try and answer, then you can have a go at asking your own.
	When the clocks went forward the other day, where did the lost hour go?
Henry:	It didn't really go anywhere
	You can't change time
	You can't make it go slower or faster
	You can't stop time
	If you didn't have any clocks time would still go on

George:	You could use sun dials they are rocks that tell you the time
F:	But what if there are no sun dials?
Henry:	Look at the sun
Lavelle:	But it might be a cloudy day?
Abbie:	If we didn't have any clocks people wouldn't know what time to go to work or cook dinner
Tilly:	I would know to go to bed at night time because my body would be tired
F:	If all clocks stopped at 2am would time stand still?
Henry:	No because time can't stop
Lavelle:	Everyone on the planet would freeze and it would repeat again and again
Henry:	I disagree, it couldn't not unless you made an invention that did
George:	There are stories where time can repeat itself
F:	Is that possible?
George:	You sometimes think time goes on and on
Henry:	If the clocks stopped then time would still carry on, clocks are only there to tell us we what the time is
Madison:	Time goes quickly that means you are having a good time
F:	Does it really travel at different times?
Madison:	No it just feels like it
Henry:	When the clocks went forward time didn't go anywhere because 3 am was actually . . . it's a bit daft because it doesn't change time. It's only clocks. Time is not clocks, that's just a machine
Henry:	Has time always happened? Will there ever be an end to time?
Henry:	Well the world will come to an end one day which is in like a million years
F:	But will time end too?
Henry:	No, because everything goes on and on and on but there could be an end in a thousand gazillion years but I don't know because I can't get myself from this time all the way to there and because I don't know how to make the things that do that and besides why would I want to go forwards or backwards in time?
Lavelle:	I would like to go back so I could have more time on the Nintendo Wii
Henry:	I would like to go all the way back
Abbie:	To dinosaur times?
George:	Or when the meteor hit?
F:	All the way back? Where did time begin?

Henry:	Well once there was no darkness no light no nothing just a void
F:	Is a void something or nothing?
Henry:	Well it's just a name there's nothing really there. But it has no edge or middle. Let me carry on telling you. . . . Then something strange happened . . . a whirling began, it got bigger and bigger then time began
F:	How did something come out from nothing though?
Henry:	I don't know, I would have to go back to before time began to figure that out
	I will discover that one day. I have two more years than my brother because I'm younger than him to figure that out.
F:	Ok so we are going to create our own philosophical questions today. I am going to get the concept cards out and you are going to ask a question that nobody knows the answer to. Try and make your questions as hard as you can by asking yourselves the next question too. Our challenge today is to listen to everybody's question and give them one extra question to make them think harder

The children's questions were:

Lavelle:	**How do we know we are not robots?**
Maddy:	**Why is the world so small from the universe?**
Abbie:	**Are there more planets than we think and could there be aliens?**
Henry:	**Why did time happen and will it end?**
Olivia:	**Why is the sun yellow?**
Tilly:	**How do we know what is yellow?**
F:	If you are blind is there such a thing as yellow? How do you know what yellow is if you have never seen it?
Tilly:	We could describe it as bright
F:	But you don't know what bright is either
Tilly:	That's too tricky
Freya:	**Why do dogs have fur?**
F:	If we took all the fur off would it still be a dog?
Freya:	Maybe it's still a dog because you bought it so you know it hasn't changed
Maddy:	Unless someone swaps it in the night
F:	Would you know then?
Freya:	Well it might not bark properly
Abbie:	Or it might be a robot dog like Lavelle's question!
George:	I have a question that's puzzling me; how do clocks tell the time if they are man-made? A man must have to put his memory

	into the clock so it knows what is one minute or one second but how does he ever know that in the first place?
F:	George's question was about time and man putting his memory into the clock. Can George explain that a bit more?
George:	Well clocks are manmade. I need to know how he knows what time is?
Henry:	Well a minute is 60 seconds and . . .
F:	Ok so this is the 1st man making the 1st ever clock. He is going to invent the first ever time telling machine . . . How does he know what one minute looks like?
Henry:	He counted 1, 2, 3
F:	Did he invent the 'second'? Did he invent counting as well, give it a name like second?
Lavelle:	He could have looked it up on the internet
Abbie:	But Lavelle, there are no clocks how can there be internet?
F:	Does a clock think for itself?
George:	No, if a clock thinks for himself it could be a disaster; it could come alive and run away It could change itself from 1 o'clock to 12 o'clock
F:	But how does it know what time it should be?
George:	Clocks are just like a mystery, they kind of have to do as they are told
Henry:	I think time decided time
George:	So our next question could be 'did time decide time?'
Henry:	How did time happen and will it end?
F:	That's already 2 much more thoughtful questions. Well done
Henry:	But will time carry on?
F:	Lavelle's question was how do we know that people are not robots? Any there more questions about this?
Lavelle:	Well my mum has cut herself because she bled and robots can't born another robot they have metal tummies
F:	How do we know mums aren't robots?
Freya:	Maybe it's a zip up costume?
Henry:	How do we know there's no such thing a as robots with realistic false blood?
F:	Good point Henry, could they ever make a robot that's so like a human in every way?
Henry:	A cyborg is a robot that looks like a human, like an android
Lavelle:	You could design a person but a robot would not be the same it would have gas and electricity and have buttons and stuff
F:	Would it have its own memories?
Lavelle:	It could have

It would have to have a robot brain

F: Is that the same?

Lavelle: No, well you could take a human brain out and put it in a robot that's the only way. I wouldn't like that

F: How do you know that that hasn't already happened?

Lavelle: Well an x-ray could tell

George: I know that I'm not a cyborg because I have wobbly teeth

Henry: But how do we know robots aren't designed to replicate wobbly teeth?

Philosophy club aged 5–7 years

This group of children extended the discussion from this work on questioning into a mini topic on robots. These questions show the depth of thinking about the nature of identity and what it means to not be human.

Case study

Robot blueprints

We created drawings and diagrams to design a robot. The children were then asked to create questions about each other's robots

Questions raised through dialogue about our robot inventions:

- If a robot cries when it burns itself cooking, is it really crying?
- Do you have to be human to cry?
- Would robots do evil things if they were programmed to do everything?
- Does a robot think for itself?
- Should humans make money from making robots do the work?
- Should robots get paid for their work?
- Is turning a robot off the same as killing it?
- How is a robot that washes clothes different to a washing machine?
- Is there a difference between a machine and a robot?
- Do robots have brains?
- How do we know if a robot has a brain?
- Do brains have to have learning in them?
- Can we teach robots to learn?
- If a robot has a memory circuit built in, can it remember things?
- Is this a real memory?
- What is a real memory?
- How can robots remember when they never grow up?
- If a computer remembers what we type does it have a memory?
- If our brain is made of electrical signals are we like machines?
- Does a robot have a personality?
- Is your personality part of your brain or your body?
- Can robots have babies?

Reflecting on the role of the facilitator

- Have your ideas about philosophical issues changed as you worked through this chapter?
- Have you shared any of these activities with colleagues, friends or family?
- Have your opinions of the validity of children's ideas changed?
- Have you allowed time to immerse yourselves in quality picture books?
- Has this changed the way you wish to resource your setting?
- How will you ensure that this methodology will extend beyond specific P4C sessions?

4

Creating Philosophical Thinkers

Chapter Outline

Setting the ground rules for philosophical enquiries

When we, as facilitators, have become accustomed to the nature of philosophical concepts and purposeful questioning, we can work with the children in a way that becomes more philosophical. The children need to be ready to develop the skills that underpin enquiry.

In any form of enquiry, it is important to establish the ground rules for dialogue, communication and understanding. The skills we aim to develop are all reliant on the ability of the children to listen and communicate as a community. When young children come into the educational setting, the rules become very different. Suddenly they are asked to share their voice with 20 or more others. They are expected to justify their ideas and develop cohesion in these ideas. When we introduce the thinking rules from week 1, we are telling our children that this is how school works. If education is a community to which we want them to belong for the next few years, we must ensure that all children have ownership of these rules.

The thinking bridge – A visual code of conduct

From week 1 in the classroom, we create a visual thinking bridge that will help us get from one land to another over a turbulent sea (often filled with man-eating sea slugs for dramatic effect).

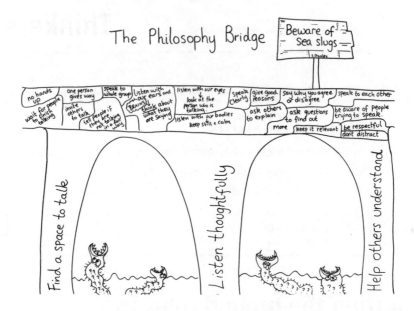

The bridge has three supports to hold it up. Each represents a thinking rule. The part of the bridge we walk across is built up of many wooden slats or stones that represent what we think those three rules actually mean. If the bridge supports are fragile, then the whole bridge becomes wobbly and we may be in danger of falling . . . and nobody wants to be eaten by a sea slug do they?

The three supports are:

- Find a space to talk
- Listen thoughtfully
- Help each other understand.

In order to build the footpath across the bridge, we must first talk about what we think, understand and believe these rules mean to us and what these rules look, sound and feel like.

Bridge support 1 – What is 'Talk into a space'?

In day-to-day conversation, human beings do not use hands up. Our children do not employ the hands-up method in the playground, the cinema or around the dinner table. When children first start to talk, we teach them through communication what conversation is. We pause after speaking to allow space for a baby to babble. We respond and so on. As children grow and become more egocentric, we remind them that it is not polite to interrupt or talk over others. In the school environment, a hands-up approach may be practical but it is also highly problematic. Who chooses who has the right to speak next? What happens to the thought process of the child with his or her hand up? What about those children who never think they have the answer? And just how representative of natural dialogue is this?

We should instead learn together how this conversation can happen in a group. We practice games and activities together that illustrate the importance of turn taking. For examples of games and activities, see *But Why?* (Stanley and Bowkett 2004). We draw attention to times when speaking is chaotic and we stop it. We remind children that we cannot operate and move on in our thinking if we do not speak into a space. This does take time but is well worth the effort. Children eventually take over facilitation of their dialogue and notice when others are trying to speak or dominate the speaking. They are given permission to say to each other, 'you have done lots of talking already' or 'what do you think (named child)?' or 'I need to finish what I am saying.'

In my classroom, we talked together about what the 'talk into a space' support meant. We came up with the following guidelines:

- No hands up
- Wait for people to finish what they are saying
- Invite others to talk
- If more than one person talks at the same time, then one person has to give way
- Tell people if they are not talking fairly
- Speak to the whole group (not just your neighbour).

Bridge support 2 – What is 'Listen thoughtfully?'

The middle bridge support deals with understanding about what it means to listen thoughtfully.

There is a big difference between hearing and listening. Listening can very easily become a passive exercise. We want to ensure that philosophy or enquiry-based learning engages children in active listening. This involves recognition that we are listening for a reason, for example, to find ways to move the thinking on.

It is through listening that we learn to understand what others think or believe. Active, reflective listening involves the ability to decode, interpret and understand what others say. When we listen in this way, we are also reflecting on what we ourselves say. We hear our ideas with a different mindset. Speaking aloud our words and then critically listening to them allow us to check for clarification and consistency in our thinking. This form of listening is also empathic listening. It requires listening not just to words but acknowledging feelings. This is, of course, a vital skill in philosophical understanding. We are listening to and feeling things that are important, and through active listening, these thoughts are represented, respected and valued. We think about listening as active because it is not just our ears that hear words, our brains have to process the words, understand and then put meaning to them. We also use our eyes and bodies in the listening process.

In the classroom, I ask the children to experience what it feels like when people do not give us eye contact. I ask them to turn away from people or fidget when they talk and then we think and talk about how this makes us feel. We then concentrate on how to let people know that we are listening; we practice common classroom games and activities that require eye contact, activities where body language and gesture are employed and face-to-face interaction is required.

The negotiated requirements for good listening recorded on our bridge are:

Listen with our brains – think about what people say
Listen with our eyes – look at the person talking
Listen with our bodies – keep calm and still.

Bridge support 3 – What does 'Helping others understand' look like?

The third support holding our bridge up is helping others understand.

This is the metaphorical support that focuses on development of philosophical rigour. Philosophy is merely a conversation without this element of logical reasonableness and pursuit of understanding. Understanding is supported by peer engagement in peer groups. As adults, we know that understanding and creativity flourish when we can bounce ideas and thoughts off each other. This interaction with our peers leads to deeper exploration. It allows us to refer back to our own thinking and that of others. Without checking back, we cannot productively move forward.

For deeper understanding, we must ensure that we ask for clarification of ideas that confuse us or do not seem relevant. Often in enquiry, children are allowed to 'ramble' because practitioners fear it may lower the child's self-esteem to stop them. Rambling should not be tolerated; instead, the child should be steered towards ensuring his or her ideas are relevant. We can teach our children to respond to ramblings with statements, such as, 'I'm not sure I understand'; facilitators can ask 'how this is relevant?' We must consider whether these ramblings are productive; is the child merely unaware of what the group is trying to say? Repeat the preceding question or idea and ask them to stop and think about their answer again.

Philosophical enquiry is concerned with establishing a shared understanding, and for an enquiry to be successful, the whole community should take responsibility. They should use the language of agreement and disagreement in a reasonable manner. The results of an enquiry are entirely reliant on good facilitation not just from the adults. The children themselves should develop the community understanding through questioning of each other's ideas.

The rules for understanding have been negotiated as follows:

- Speak clearly – look up
- Give good reasons
- Ask others to explain
- Say why you agree or disagree
- Ask questions to find out more
- Keep it relevant
- Speak to each other – use names
- Be aware of others trying to speak
- Be respectful – do not laugh at people's ideas
- Do not distract others from the enquiry.

You may wish to use the blank format photocopiable sheet with your own groups of children. Allowing them to explore how these ground rules work will mean that they have responsibility for making their enquiries successful. Display the bridge in the classroom and refer the children to their agreements on thinking behaviours if/when necessary. The thinking bridge is not exclusively beneficial for philosophy sessions but for behaviour in any classroom where thinking underpins play, dialogue and peer interaction.

Once the ground rules have been established, we have taken the first step in introducing the skills involved in philosophical thinking. The skills and rules for enquiry are very closely linked as they form the backbone of the disciplines required.

The traditional model of P4C requires that children should be able to ask questions, justify their answers and work together Socratically. However, it is unreasonable to expect both child and inexperienced facilitator to instantly meet this expectation. It is necessary to first analyse what steps we have to take on the path to successful, exciting and enjoyable enquiries.

We do not expect our children to write novels without first teaching them the basic skills necessary to do so and thus we need to break down the enquiry process into progressive manageable skills.

These skills developed by Maria Cornish and Sara Stanley of children thinking are called the philosophy building blocks (see also *But Why?* – Stanley and Bowkett 2004). These building blocks have since been put into a more progressive order, related not to age but to experience levels. The building blocks still form the basis for planning, reviewing and assessing philosophical progress.

The activities and experiences that we provide for the children will develop philosophical understanding. We should try out enquiries with picture books in the traditional model every so often so that we can see which skills the children have acquired and which they still need to develop. Using the building blocks with the children is a productive multi-method assessment tool. They can be used for individual assessment, peer assessment and group assessment. The facilitator can look at the skills being used as an evaluation tool and plan for the next steps in philosophical development.

What are the philosophical skills in progressive order?

Making and justifying choices

- Children understand rules of enquiry
- Children can make a decision and remember what it is
- Children can give reasons for their choices
- Children understand whether they agree or disagree with other ideas including their own
- Children can find a space to talk.

Working with the concepts

- Children are introduced to concepts
- Children build up a concept bank
- Children can identify concepts within the stimulus
- Children can see connections between concepts
- Children can ask questions based on concepts.

Questions and connections

- Children can ask a question relevant to stimulus
- Children can understand good questions for enquiry
- Children can match questions to concepts
- Children can connect questions in relation to concepts
- Children can see more than one concept within same question.

Enquiry and dialogue

- Children can understand concepts within the dialogue
- Children can vote for a question they have interest in
- Children can build on an idea
- Children can facilitate their own enquiries
- Children can point out contradictions
- Children can think logically.

Using the daily question board to develop progression of skills

In order to create the sort of statements and questions that we use to develop critical thinking skills, we have to hold in our minds the thoughtfulness of the big issues of the previous chapters.

Why use a question board?

Big concepts start with small moments. Small moments end in big concepts.

The daily question board is used to encourage my children to start each session with an idea or question. This sends a very strong message to the children and their parents that they are entering a thinking space.

The nature of the question board stimuli are playful in nature, often based on fairy tales and ideas that appeal to young children. The expectation, however, is that thinking is something that requires communication and its status in my setting is paramount.

The question board thoughts are displayed on the classroom philosophy display board.

How we use the question board

When the children come into the session with their parents/carers, they find their names and register their attendance by placing their name on the board under the heading that indicates their answer or idea about the question.

I greet the children and adults at the board and model language, such as, 'why do you think that? Do you think the same as your grown up or do you disagree? I wonder what would happen if . . .?'

The parents pick up this way of interacting with the children very quickly, and it is heartening to see so many parents show an interest in their child's opinions in an educational situation. This also sends a very powerful message to parents that we value their children's ideas and place emphasis on their intellectual development as well.

The activities on the board follow the progression of skills. I start with making and justifying choices. I work through the cards in this category every day until I feel the children are working well within the skill.

The following set of photocopiable activities should last for a whole school year but you can also add your own ideas to the bank or the ideas of your pupils. The cards that I display on the question board can also be used as a stimulus for a short enquiry-based activity. The question or idea can also be referred to at various times of the day, such as snack time. Often the children refer to the question board cards during carpet times making connections between things we might be discussing or just reminding me of what they thought.

Sometimes, children and/or parents might approach me and say that they could not make a decision. On these opportunities, we take the problem to the whole group and ask whether we can discuss it to help people make a decision. I do not allow children to put their name in the middle; instead, I encourage them to take the role of a scientist. Often we do not know which answer to give, we may not have enough information to make a decision or we may fear giving the wrong answer. In this case, we have to go with one decision treating it in the same way that we would when we were creating a hypothesis in a science experiment; make a decision, see what happens and then adjust our thinking based on the result, if necessary. In philosophy, we should embrace indecision as a way forward. When this happens, we can encourage dialogue and debate about the issue, offering the puzzled child opportunities to talk it through and become an active participant in an investigative thinking process.

Resourcing the daily question board

Progressive question board activities

These activities follow the progression of skills that we will be developing in the classroom over the year. The daily exercises consolidate and compliment the thinking process that we aim to embed in our children's play and thinking.

Activity: Making and remembering a choice – You choose . . .

You will need a card to represent each item mentioned in the lists below. Each list is also available on the companion website for you to print off or refer to online.

You will need to choose two cards. It does not have to be the two presented/suggested here. They can of course be mixed and matched. Place one card on one side of the board and one on the other; children should be encouraged to put their name under the label of their choice after an adult has read it to them and they should be encouraged to say why.

In the trees or underground?
No ears or no eyes?
Presents or cuddles?
Scary kittens or happy monsters?
Prison or hospital?
Crowded or deserted?
Purple face or green toes?
Sing or shout?
Spiders or snakes?
Sweets or magazines?
Indoors or outdoors?
Music or painting?
Noise or quiet?
Seaside or zoo?
Ship or castle?
King or clown?
Roundabouts or swings?
Book or film?
Dance or sing?
Frog prince or beast?
Dragon or witch?
Tiny elephants or giant ants?
Claws or paws?
Pink or blue?
Teddy or treasure?
School or television?
Mud or puddles?
Worms or snail slime?
Cold soup or hot ice cream?
Tadpoles on toast or spider pie?
Spaceship or submarine?
Father Christmas or tooth fairy?
Strawberries or chocolate?
Monkey or lion?

Time travels forwards or backwards?
Magic beans or money?
Big Bad Wolf or troll?
Robot or teacher?

Activity: Making a choice and justifying it – YES or NO?

You will need one statement label saying 'Yes because . . .' and one that says 'No because . . .'

Sweets for breakfast, lunch and tea
Snowmen in summer
Six hands
No nursery
Boys in pink dresses
Girls playing football
Tiny elephants
Sleep all day
Stay awake all night
Lollipop trees
Flying cars
Chocolate rain
No money
Talking chickens
Giant babies
Green skin
Hot ice cream
Smelly kittens
No girls
Magic wands for everyone
Children in charge
Birthdays every day
Dinosaur eggs
Everyone looks the same
Always happy

Activity: Making and justifying a choice with extended reasoning and creative thinking – 'What Ifs'. Would it be a Good Thing or a Bad Thing if . . .?

You will need one statement presented on each statement card. One label that reads 'Good because. . .' and one that reads 'Bad because. . .'

We could hear people's thoughts
We grew 1 cm a day
If humans walked on four legs
There was a cure for everything
All lies came true
Choose our own families
Dinosaurs still roamed the land
Everything in the world was edible
Writing was never invented
Every country was an island
All books were destroyed
All history was a lie and time was just repeating itself
Time went backwards
Babies hatched out of eggs
Nobody was allowed to own anything
We could swap brains with our friends
Machines could think for themselves
There was no such thing as prison
Kittens grew as big as elephants

Activity: Making decisions based on more than two choices – Would you rather?

You will need one statement card. Each statement card should have three options for the child to choose between. You may alternatively wish to use three post-its with simple illustrations or wording for each option. Children should place their name under one of these three choices. These cards are also available online for you to print off.

Would you rather be locked in . . .?
a) A bird cage?
b) A dungeon?
c) A school?

Would you rather be born again as . . .?
a) A bird?
b) A tortoise?
c) A lion?

Would you rather live with . . .?
a) The Big Bad Wolf?
b) Goldilocks?
c) The seven dwarves?

Would you rather live without . . .?
a) Your hands?
b) Your eyes?
c) Your ears?

Would you rather the only rule in the world should be . . .?
a) Everybody must only ever wear school uniform?
b) Everybody must smile at all times?
c) Nobody is allowed to spend any money?

Would you rather people were not allowed to . . .?
a) Be angry?
b) Be sad?
c) Be silly?

Would you rather look like . . .?
a) A kitten?
b) A monkey?
c) A frog?

Would you rather live . . .?
a) On the moon?
b) In a jungle?
c) Underground?

Would you rather be . . .?
a) As small as an ant?
b) As big as a giant?
c) As scary as a monster?

Would you rather have the powers of . . .?
a) Spiderman?
b) A werewolf?
c) Father Christmas?

Would you rather sit in a bath of . . .?
a) Baked beans?
b) Wriggly worms?
c) Stinging nettles?

Would you rather be left in a room full of . . .?
a) Boring grownups?
b) Crying babies?
c) Barking dogs?

Would you rather invent . . .?
a) Cure for the common cold?
b) A tree that grew chocolate coins?
c) An animal that could talk?

Would you rather meet . . .?
a) Your great great grandmother?
b) Your great great grandchild?
c) Yourself?

Would you rather have two . . .?
a) Mothers?
b) Brains?
c) Lives?

Would you rather buy . . .?
a) A book that could talk?
b) A carpet that could fly?
c) A bag of sweets that never empties?

Would you rather have a robot that could . . .?
a) Do all your homework?
b) Tidy your bedroom?
c) Eat all your vegetables?

Would you rather have . . .?
a) A living dinosaur?
b) A purse that never emptied?
c) A key to a secret door?

Would you rather be . . .?
a) A teacher?
b) A clown?
c) A doctor?

Would you rather have . . .?
a) No house?
b) No money?
c) No friends?

Would you rather have a million . . .?
a) Pounds?
b) Friends?
c) Toys?

What would you rather be chased by . . .?
a) An angry wasp?
b) A grumpy fairy?
c) A tickle monster?

Who would you like to come to your party?
a) A burglar?
b) An alien?
c) A witch?

What would you rather look after?
a) A baby Giant?
b) A giant baby?
c) A tiny elephant?

What day would you like it to be?
a) Easter?
b) Christmas?
c) Your birthday?

What would you like to do today?
a) Go on a bear hunt?
b) Go to a chocolate factory?
c) Build a snowman?

Activity: Making a choice – Using the language of enquiry – Agree/disagree

You will need one statement and one label saying 'Agree because. . .' and one 'disagree because. . .'

Animals can have dreams.
Animals should talk with human words.
Broccoli is better than chocolate.

Chocolate buttons should grow on trees.

Children are cleverer than grown-ups.

Dinosaurs are scarier than lions.

People should have four legs.

Everything in the world should be pink.

People should have wings.

Sun is better than rain.

Tigers should live in zoos.

We should always do what we are told to do.

We learn more from TV than at school.

We should share everything.

Monsters are unkind.

All books are good.

All flowers are beautiful.

Activity: Thinking again about initial answers – Alternative thinking

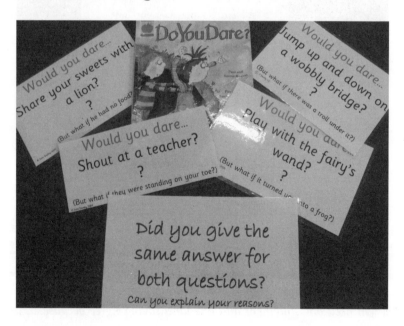

Would you dare?

*You will need one statement and one I label saying 'Yes because. . .'
and one 'No because. . .'. The statement cards are also available
online for you to print off.*

Ask the adult to read out the first part of the statement and ask their child to give an answer/reason. Then the second part of the question should be read out. Does the child still think the same? If not, why not?

Would you dare . . .?
Say 'BOO!' to a monster?
(But what if it couldn't hear?)

Would you dare . . .?
Jump up and down on a wobbly bridge?
(But what if there was a troll under it?)

Would you dare . . .?
Go through a secret door?
(But what if there was no way back?)

Would you dare . . .?
Have tea with a pirate?
(But what if it was a mummy pirate?)

Would you dare . . .?
Swim with a shark?
(But what if it was a baby one?)

Would you dare . . .?
Stroke the fluffy bunny rabbit?
(But what if it had monster teeth?)

Would you dare . . .?
Squash a scary spider?
(But what if it was the only one in the world?)

Would you dare . . .?
Shout at a teacher?
(But what if they were standing on your toe?)

Would you dare . . .?
Share your sweets with a lion?
(But what if he had no food?)

Would you dare . . .?
Play with a giant teddy bear?
(But what if it likes sitting on you?)

Would you dare . . .?
Play with a witch?
(But what if it was only a little girl or boy witch?)

Would you dare . . .?
Play with the fairy's wand?
(But what if it turned you into a frog?)

Would you dare . . .?
Play with a monster?
(But what if he had no friends?)

Would you dare . . .?
Pick a beautiful flower?
(But what if it was the last one in the world?)

Would you dare . . .?
Marry the King or Queen?
(But what if they lived in a prison?)

Would you dare . . .?
Live in a beautiful palace?
(But what if there were no doors or windows?)

Would you dare . . .?
Eat sweets every day?
(But what if it made your teeth fall out?)

Would you dare . . .?
Go into space?
(But what if the aliens were nasty?)

Would you dare . . .?
Lick a blackcurrant lollipop?
(But what if it turned your face purple?)

Would you dare . . .?
Kiss a frog?
(But what if it would turn into a prince or princess?)

Would you dare . . .?
Hold hands with a hairy monkey?
(But what if he had chickenpox?)

Would you dare . . .?
Put your hands in a mud pie?
(But what if it smelled of fish?)

Would you dare . . .?
Go into space?
(But what if the aliens were nasty?)

Would you dare . . .?
Make friends with a fairy?
(But what if she only did bad magic?)

Would you dare . . .?
Eat a worm?
(But what if it was covered in chocolate?)

Would you dare . . .?
Pick up some dinosaur poo?
(But what if it smelled like strawberry)

Would you dare . . .?
Cuddle a crocodile?
(But what if it had no teeth?)

Looking for connections

Activity: Same and different

Choose any combination of two of the Same Different Cards that you can see similarities or differences between. Make these more obvious to begin with. Ask the children to look and see whether they notice anything the same or anything different about the pictures. The cards are in the Resources section and on the companion website.

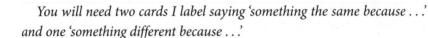

You will need two cards I label saying 'something the same because . . .' and one 'something different because . . .'

Dog
Spider
Dragon
King
Flower
Beanstalk
Giant
Alien
Gold
Key
Hat
Crown
Lolly
Banana
Prison
School
Teddy
Witch
Wand
Wolf
Sheep
Sun
Book
Sword
Cage
Chocolate

Reflective questions about how we can create philosophical thinkers

- How has the social environment of the classroom changed since setting up the rules for enquiry-based learning?
- Which expectations of philosophical behaviours do the children struggle or succeed with?
- How can you allow time to discuss daily questions in your environment?
- How can we allow time to listen to children's questions?
- How will questioning and dialogue extend into all areas of learning and teaching?
- How will questioning underpin your classroom management and curriculum development?

5
First Enquiries

Chapter Outline

Alongside working through the daily question board skill-based activities, we have a weekly philosophy session to practice these skills in more depth. These sessions start off as short 15- to 20-minute activities and build up to an hour with age and experience. The activities consolidate and reinforce the rules of enquiry and dialogue. Although when working with younger children, I often refer to them as 'philosophy games', these activities are equally as validly referred to as 'Enquiries' with older children. I have worked with children up to Key Stage 2 (ages 7–11 years) in all these activities. The difference is in the outcomes produced. The older children of course bring much more sophistication to the dialogue in terms of language and experience but it is essential that they still use these activities to build the skills needed for rigorous philosophical thinking.

First enquiry activities for all ages

The first part of this chapter demonstrates what early enquiries look like in the classroom. I have presented these case studies to inspire and motivate practitioners to have a go.

Case studies

Who has the crown?

Just before we gathered for the session, I left a small crown on the car-pet. I watched to see what would happen. As predicted, one child picked it up and put it on her head. The group gathered in the thinking circle. I reminded the children of our philosophy rules and began the enquiry.

Facilitator (F):	Oh, where did that crown come from?
Cybele:	Maybe someone brought it in?
Jessica:	It came from the Queen or a king
Henry:	It's for putting on the King's head
Millie:	You should try it on Mrs Stanley!
F:	OK, may I have it please Shauna?

(Shauna passed the crown.)

Kelsey:	It's too small for your head

(We passed the crown around the circle)

Poppy:	It does fit Kelsey
Ella:	No it doesn't, her hair sticks out
F:	Has anyone else got any ideas where it came from?
Millie:	It might be someone who lost it
Harry:	Maybe the king lost it
Tyler:	The king doesn't come to nursery though
Eva:	Or the Queen
Poppy:	It did fit Lexie well
Holly:	I don't think it will fit Henry

(The children find this funny)

F:	Oh, why are people laughing?
Kelsey:	It looks funny
Poppy:	I don't think it looks funny, it looks good
Cybele:	But his hair has gone scary
Millie:	I think it's a crown for someone with a small head
Jude:	A king lion wears it
Holly:	But lions don't wear crowns

(The children continue to pass the crown round the circle as they talk)

Catie:	It won't fit any boy
Eva:	When I grow up I will be a princess
Poppy:	Holly has been wearing the crown for a long time

Jude:	That's not fair, pass it round
Kelsey:	It looks good on Millie 'cos she's a girl
Tyler:	I think Joe looks like a Queen
Cybele:	Boys don't wear Queen crowns. They are supposed to be Kings
Poppy:	But it looks great on Jude
F:	We have a problem. How many crowns do we have?
Children:	Just one
F:	I need somebody to be the King or Queen just for today. How many people would like to be King or Queen? *(counts)* OK, I counted 15 hands but 14 people want it. I wonder why? Harry, why did you have two hands up?
Harry:	I don't know
F:	There has to be a reason
Cybele:	There shouldn't have to be a reason if you don't want to tell the reason
Millie:	Maybe he wanted to be both. One hand for a King and one for a Queen
F:	That's an interesting idea. Maybe Harry wants it most?
Harry:	Yes, can I have it?
F:	I think it is up to the group to decide. Should Harry have it?
Millie:	No. You should put some cards out and the first one to get to the picture of a 'yes' should get it
F:	Like a race?
Henry:	Yes we should have a winner who gets the crown
F:	Does anyone see any problems with that?
Ella:	We can't let a winner take it home they might forget and we only get one winner
Ryan:	But we are not allowed to run in nursery
Millie:	We could crawl there
F:	Would it be fair to the people who weren't very good at running or crawling?
Children:	No
F:	So how else can we decide?
Henry:	I should have it 'cos I wish I could have it
Holly:	That's not really fair because it's not just for Henry, it's for nursery
Poppy:	We can share, we are good at sharing
F:	I can't let you share. The rules today are that we have to decide on only one person to have the crown
Shauna:	It can't be for Holly because she already wore it for a long time
F:	We can only share it from now
Ryan:	We can't have to play with it then

Ella:	What if we accidently take it home?
Millie:	We can choose who has it if we think hard
F:	Who will choose?
Several children:	You
F:	Is it fair that I should choose?
Poppy:	We could look in a book to see who should wear it
F:	But the problem is we don't have a book that tells us that
Millie:	We should do the race
F:	But we can't run
Eva:	We can crawl
Holly:	But it would hurt our knees
F:	Someone said it looks good on Kelsey. Should she be allowed to wear it?
Cybele:	Only me and Joe can decide because nobody else can do it
Millie:	No, Mrs Stanley should do it
Poppy:	We could make another hat?
Tyler:	Can we have two kings or queens?
F:	Not really. The rule is we can only have one king or Queen. Our real Queen wears a crown, where did she get it?
Joe:	From the shops
F:	If you can buy a real crown from a shop why is there only one Queen? Can we all be a Queen if we buy a crown?
Poppy:	My mummy did for her wedding
F:	Is she the queen then?
Poppy:	No
F:	Because we can't decide should we give it to the person who has a mummy or daddy who is the real King or Queen of our country?

(Facilitator explains again what a monarch does, where they live etc.)

F:	If that is your mum or dad put your hand up so I can count
Holly:	My mum lives in a tower
Poppy:	Holly that's not the truth. Your house is near my grandma and I've seen your house, it's not a palace!
Millie:	My nanny says my mum is a Queen
Poppy:	I think Millie's mum should wear our crown. Is she picking you up today Millie? We can tell her to be Queen because if your nanny says your mum is a Queen then nannies know

People in the toy zoo

F:	We are going to do some thinking about this ok?
Child (C):	You're building a cage for the animals
F:	I'm doing a cage for the animals am I? ok . . .
C:	I know what you are doing I have thought about that
F:	OK what do you think I am doing?
C:	A cage for the animals!
F:	You as well? Put your hands up if you agree that I am making a cage for the animals
C:	No you're not – you are going to put the animals after
F:	Put the animals after?
C:	You are making a zoo!
F:	I am making a zoo? So you are looking at this and saying 'ah! Mrs Stanley is making a zoo.' What is a zoo?
C:	I went to the zoo! They have got trains! And where you can play somewhere
F:	Do all zoos have trains?
Children:	No! No!
F:	Stop, what are the rules in philosophy? You can't talk and listen unless you . . .?
Children:	Find your space!
F:	Ok so if I say to you 'what is a zoo?' what would you say?
Shauna:	It's where animals live.

F: A zoo is where animals live. OK. That is a statement.

Cybele: It's an animal's home. They live there but they don't live there all the while. They go home and live in their cage.

F: OK so they live there. But not all the time? They go home to their cage somewhere else?

Tyler: Yes. They live in a cage in Africa

F: After they've been in the zoo? Can you explain a bit more?

Tyler: Animals come from different places they can't all come home but some can

F: So some animals go to the zoo and then some animals can go home to . . .?

Tyler: Africa

Poppy: Africa or wherever their real home was

Cybele: But if they live there then they need to live there for a long time. They don't live in a house

Tyler: They do!

F: OK Tyler tell Cybele why they do live in a house

Tyler: Because they do

F: That's not a good enough reason. How do we know that they are living in a house? Are their houses the same as people houses?

Holly: No they are not. Not this house. If you have a big cat it's going to be a big pet and it can't even fit through the door

F: OK. So you are saying that animals can't live in houses?

Jude: You can have rats as pets

F: Is that to do with houses?

Jude: They can fit through the door

F: Oh I see so you are saying that you could have a small animal because it would fit through the door?

Jude: Yes. In a cage

F: Why does it have to be in cage?

Henry: Because that would run off

F: So you would keep it in a cage because it would run off?

Millie: It would get lost

F: Anyone know anything else about a zoo that we haven't talked about yet?

Ella: All zoos have flamingos

F: Do all zoos have flamingos?

Jessica: Some do. I went to Africa Alive and I saw some flamingos and they had a baby

F: Right so you might see some baby animals there. OK I am going to play my game now. You all think this is a zoo. It says 'Welcome to Wanju Zoo'. It's got some writing on it. Here's the turnstile where you pay and get your ticket

(The animals are lined up at the turnstile)

Jessica:	Why are you putting them there?
F:	You can be guessing if you like. That's part of the game
Cybele:	I think they are the first animals in
F:	They are the first animals into the zoo? And what's going to happen then when they come through the ticket office?
Holly:	How will they get them from the ticket man?
Kelsey:	Their teeth!
F:	So they are going to get their ticket from the ticket man with their teeth? Ok that's a guess
Catie:	I know what the elephant will do – he'll get his trunk
F:	So the elephants going to use his trunk? You think they are all waiting to buy a ticket?
Poppy:	I think they are going to go in their pen
Harry:	But the lion will probably eat it
F:	Eat what?
Harry:	The ticket
F:	The lion will probably eat the ticket?
Holly:	You've got to put him in his cage now!
F:	Now?
Chidren:	Yes!
F:	Well he has got to wait his turn hasn't he? It's not his turn yet
Cybele:	Just get him and put him in his cage
F:	What just get him? How will I lift him? I'd need a crane to lift a lion!
Tyler:	I can, look!
F:	I think he's got to stay there in the queue. This is the next part of the game – are you watching?

(The facilitator puts the people in the cages)

Ella:	Why are you putting people in the cage?
F:	You can guess
Ryan:	Because the lion will eat them?
Luke:	Maybe because they are waiting for a pet?
F:	What did you say Luke?
Luke:	The lion might bite them?
F:	So why are they in the cages then, how will that help?
Luke:	Because the lion wants to eat them
F:	But why would they go in a cage if a lion wants to eat them?
Luke:	If they were real people and they knew that a lion wanted to eat them it would be tricky to get them in the cage
Millie:	But the lion was only pretend

F:	Well then why are they in a cage?
Poppy:	Because it's part of our game!
F:	It's part of our game but what are we trying to think about? Anybody see any problems?
Poppy:	Maybe it's a different kind of zoo where animals pet people
F:	Animals come to the zoo to pet and look after people?
Poppy:	Well the giraffe and the elephant and zebra would but not the lion
F:	So what's different about the lion?
Kelsey:	Because he might eat people
F:	So who can come into the zoo then? Ryan can you come and choose an animal to come and buy a ticket

(Ryan chooses the zebra)

F:	What would the zebra say?
Ryan:	Please may I have a ticket?
F:	Can this zebra talk?
Children:	No! He would say brrrrr!
F:	And if he said brrrrr! Would we understand what he was saying?
Poppy:	What if the person at the ticket machine wouldn't know what the zebra was saying? But if they did then he could go through
F:	Can we understand what animals are saying?
Millie:	Some people can and some people can't
Cybele:	The animals might not understand what the people are saying
Poppy:	If some people could talk zebra then they won't let them go in
F:	So some people might be able to talk zebra? How do we know whether we can understand animals or not?
Millie:	They won't understand. The zebra won't understand what the people are saying. All of the animals in the zoo won't talk. When I went to the zoo the animals didn't even talk to me
F:	Who said that animals do understand people?
Ella:	I did. My cat understands me
F:	Does your cat understand what you are saying?
Ella:	Erm no
F:	Who's got a dog?
Henry:	I have
F:	Does it understand you? If you say come here does your dog come here?
Henry:	Yes but I always wave my hand my dog comes to me
F:	So it understands you?

Henry:	It understands me in a different way. It knows it wants to come here
Ryan:	If I say 'sit' to my dog he will sit
Ella:	If I say that to my cat he won't sit because he's not interested
F:	So does the dog understand you?
Ryan:	The dog does but the cat doesn't
F:	How does a dog understand you and a cat doesn't?
Cybele:	They can't because they can't even talk. They have got too many legs and we have got just two legs. They can scratch but we can't
Jessica:	But when we were small we crawled on four legs
Poppy:	They have got two legs. The front ones are actually their arms but they are walking on them.
F:	Jessica said that's what we used to do when we were small. So were we animals?
Poppy:	I crawled
F:	Does that mean you were an animal?
Children:	No!
F:	OK, shall we do the next part of the story then? All the lions are coming in; we have got over the barrier of communicating. We are going to remove the ticket office so we don't have the problem of communicating. What's the problem? Are you scared?
Cybele:	The lion might eat all the people in the land! He might eat the zebra?
F:	That's a problem?
F:	OK I tell you what. (*moves lion and pretends to be lion*) 'I am going to go and see these people over here, and these people over here.' Anybody else allowed in?
Poppy:	Zebra is allowed in

(The children take it in turns to put the rest of the animals inside the zoo. All animals are placed away from the lion)

F:	Nobody has gone near lion! Why is lion all on his own?
Tyler:	Because he's probably scared of the other animals
Holly:	The other animals are scared of the lion! Maybe they know that the lion is going to eat them!
Cybele:	But what if they didn't? If they didn't know he was a lion they might be friendly. When you are nice to them they don't even hurt you.
Luke:	Or the lion is going to eat them all up
F:	Is the only problem here the lion? So are there any other problems with this zoo?
Ella:	There's another problem

F:	What's the other problem?
Ella:	The zoo is a bit messy
F:	In what way?
Ella:	Because the carrots are everywhere and the milk churn is everywhere
F:	What do you think they are for?
Tyler:	They are for eating
F:	Who can eat them?
Luke:	The lions, the animals
Poppy:	Well I eat carrots they are nice
F:	Poppy is going to take the carrots and feed the animals in the zoo

(Poppy picks up the carrots but starts feeding the people)

Cybele:	They are not the animals! They are the people!
F:	But they are in the cage?
Cybele:	But there is the animals. The ones outside the cages
F:	So these people aren't animals?
Jessica:	No those are people
Poppy:	Well we are actually animals
Cybele:	We are not!
Poppy:	We are animals but we are just cleverer than the other animals
Ella:	But we are not called animals
Tyler:	We are not even animals we are humans
F:	OK Poppy what makes something an animal? What is the difference between people and animals?
Poppy:	People are clever. Lions aren't as clever as people but we are still animals but we are just cleverer and we are animals like these
Millie:	Maybe they think we are animals?
Holly:	We are not animals
Ryan:	I can talk like an animal
Jessica:	Because maybe they don't talk yet?
F:	So do you think the animals think that we are animals Jessica?
Jessica:	No But animals don't know that we are animals
F:	Do you think it would be a good thing if animals went for a day out at the zoo to see other animals?
Luke:	No! It wouldn't
F:	Would you go to a zoo that had people in the cages?
Henry:	Yes!
F:	Why?
Henry:	Police can trap people in cages. The police would take the animals out and put the people back in the cages

F: Do you think these people are bad people?

Cybele: They are in prison! Put all the people in there

(All the people are placed in one cage)

F: There's a lot of people in there now is that OK?

Millie: No the people are on people because what if they get squished

F: But that doesn't matter they are all baddies now aren't they?

Kelsey: But if they are gooder maybe they will get out?

Cybele: It's even a better idea to put them in the lion's tummy

F: They should be eaten? Because they are baddies?

Millie: Some people try to not do things but they just do.

F: So you think that people don't do things on purpose?

Holly: They don't know what is what.

Cybele: The work man will come and try and get all the people out and put the animals back in.

Election day – 6 May 2010 General election at Sparhawk Infant and Nursery School – Nursery class
Morning session

Twenty-two children aged between 3.8 and 4.7 years

The children were informed that they would be given the chance to vote for a new leader of the Nursery – we explained that three staff would pretend to be three different animals for the duration of the election process. All the staff pre-prepared a manifesto for their animal.

- **Mrs Lion**

Manifesto – Vote for lion! I am strong and fierce. I will protect everyone from danger. I will roar loudly at people who hurt or scare you.

- **Ms Monkey**

Manifesto – Vote for fun! Monkey thinks we should have no rules and have fun and games all day. We should all do what we want, when we want.

- **Mr Elephant**

Vote for Elephant because I am old and wise! I will never forget to take care of anyone. I am so big nobody would dare to hurt us and on a hot day I would cool us down with water from my trunk. I have big ears so I am good at listening to you.

Each candidate read his or her manifesto and asked for questions from the floor.

Children's questions to elephant

Question to elephant – but wouldn't you find it hard not to stand on the children as you are so big?

Elephant:	No some of my best friends are actually mice. I am a very careful creature.
Child:	Can I have a ride on you, Elephant?
Lion:	But won't you be worried you'd fall off, he is very high up you know.
Child:	Will you share your apples with us?
Elephant:	Oh yes I will make sure everyone eats fruit and vegetables all day
Lion:	But you don't eat any meat, people need to eat meat don't they? That is the healthiest food.
Monkey:	No I think we should eat sweets all day and bananas and ice cream because they are the nicest foods
Lion:	Does anyone have any questions for me?

Elephant:	Yes can I ask whether if you get hungry you might be tempted to eat children? Because they are the right size for a tasty snack.
Lion:	Oh no, I promise never to do that
Elephant:	But how do we know we can trust you?
Lion:	A king can always be trusted
Monkey:	Does anyone have any questions for me?
Lion:	If you are silly I am worried the children might get hurt. Would you look after them?
Monkey:	Oh no, they will be too busy playing and having fun. I will be busy too but it won't matter because we will be having such a great time.

Voting

The children were then given ballot papers with pictures of the animals on them and the process was explained.

The children completed and posted their voting papers and we then chose some returning officers to count and record the votes. Monkey won by a majority.

At the end of the session, I called all parent/carers in and explained what we had been doing and asked for their permission to put monkey in charge for an hour the next day. I assured them that lion and elephant would of course be there to help if needed. The parents agreed.

The next day

The monkey announced that her reign would begin and reminded the children that there would be no rules and everybody could do as he or she pleased.

After the hour, the children came together to discuss what had happened and how they felt about it.

Children's responses:

Ella:	I got cross with monkey she didn't listen to me. I got cross 'cos she was naughty and stopped me coming down the slide
Yasmin:	Yes, Monkey came down the slide backwards and then fell asleep and nobody else could get down the slide
Ashley:	I fell over and she didn't even help me get Mr Bump
Kennedy:	Yes she was naughty to do that
F:	Was monkey a good leader do you think?
Sky:	I didn't have fun. She's not a good leader
Maddison:	I wanted Mrs D back again
Tayla:	She wouldn't play with me
Lucy:	She didn't listen, she was too busy on the climbing frame
Freya:	When we fell over monkey wasn't looking
Dylan:	And she didn't open the bike shed for me when I wanted the lawnmower
Ryan:	I don't think I want monkey every day she wasn't kind
Joseph:	We couldn't do everything for ourself
Yasmin:	I had no one to have fun with everyone was busy playing with monkey
Tayla:	I didn't like the game because I had to remember to call Mrs D 'Monkey' I didn't like that
F:	Shall we vote again with our choosing cards? Who thinks monkey can be leader again tomorrow?

Only four children say yes. I asked them to say why.

Kennedy:	I liked having fun
Jorja:	It was good, we could do whatever we wanted
F:	What did you do that you had always wanted to do then?
Tilly:	I went down the slide backwards
	I asked Poppy whether she had done anything different when monkey was in charge?
Poppy:	I painted my face blue with the paintbrush, I wanted to know what it felt like to have a blue face. I didn't like it I washed it

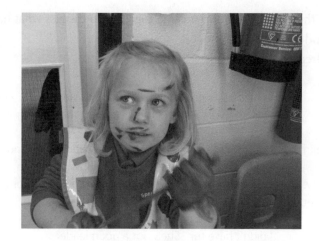

F: Did anyone else have fun?
Taylor: Yes we did we played football
F: Was it different playing today because you had no rules?
Taylor: Yes I scored more goals
F: But James got hurt didn't he?
Taylor: Yes I tackled him
Dylan: When monkey came to play football she cheated. She didn't give me the ball. The game was spoiled
Joe: And we had to throw the boat in the bin because someone broke it
F: Was it a bit like cheating when you didn't have being kind to each rules in football?
Taylor: No I think no rules is better
F: Is that why you have voted for monkey again?
Taylor: Yes
F: Can anybody think of any problems if monkey is in charge of nursery forever?
Jorja: She can't do snack properly because she can't cut apples
Shauna: And she won't do the hello song
Olivia: It's not nice not to say hello
Ashley: She too naughty
F: OK who would you like to be in charge tomorrow lion or elephant?

The children voted by moving to sit with either 'Lion' or 'Elephant'. Lion won the majority.

F: Why did you choose lion?
Gemma: Because lions are strong
Kennedy: They will roar at bad things

F:	Why did some of you choose elephant?
Tilly:	So I can have a ride
Olivia:	And I want to be noisy and squirt people with my trunk

The parents were informed of the children's decision and the exercise repeated with me in charge as Lion the next day.

Children's responses

F:	What happened when Lion was in charge?
Ryan:	You didn't scare me
Yasmin:	It was good. We didn't get hurt today
Ashley:	I did
	I falled off the scooter
F:	What happened?
Ashley:	You put a plaster on
F:	Was that me or Mrs Lion?
Ashley:	You
F:	Did anyone else see Lion today?
Dylan:	I sawed lion growl
F:	What was Lion growling at?
James:	When people pushed in to go to the toilet
F:	What happened?
James:	They said sorry
F:	So was Lion in charge today or me?

The majority of children decided it was me. It seems they found it difficult to distinguish between me and a Lion who ensured things remained fair and calm. Perhaps it was my poor acting?

Invisible pet

I filled an empty cardboard box with a furry blanket and asked the children if they would like to hold my new pet that I had brought in to school today.

Ella: I just want to see it
Catie: No . . .
F: Why not Catie?
Catie: I don't like to . . . I don't love it

I showed the children the contents of the empty box, talking to the 'pet' in a soothing voice while doing so. I asked the children to indicate who had seen my pet. The majority said no. Only three children said yes at this point.

F: So do you think you'd like to play with it now?
Millie: Yes, but it's so small
Ella: I do
F: But you said you didn't see it Ella?
Ella: it was deep down I think
Shauna: You said you couldn't see it so why do you want to play with it?
Shauna: I want to see it again
F: I'm going to let him have a little sleep now because he's very tired. Maybe you can see him later.

The children all went off to play. A while later I called Shauna over and asked if she'd like to play with the pet now. She said yes. We went over to the box and I declared dramatically that he had escaped. Shauna excitedly told several children so I gathered them all together on the carpet to explain. I asked the children whether they could help to find him as he must be somewhere in the room. All the children without exception joined in for several minutes. There were cries of 'I've found it', 'Here it is' and 'Look I've found something'.

Many brought back stuffed toys or nursery equipment which we put in the middle of the circle when we reconvened.

F: Can you tell me what you found?
Ella: A pet, a small, tiny thing
Ryan: A big thing. I found it under the table

F:	How do you know that is my pet?
Millie:	It is the one that was under the covers
Kelsey:	I just saw an old blanket
Millie:	It was under the covers that's why we couldn't see him
Jessica:	I found this pet (*a nursery toy*)
F:	Is this my pet?
Jess:	No, it's mine it has my name on
Shauna:	I found this (*a book*)
Ryan:	No that's a book Shauna
F:	Can a book be a pet if we talk to it?
Harry:	No, we can't take a book for a walk
Millie:	It can't walk
F:	I don't think any of these things you've found are my pet, was there really a pet in my box do you think?

All these people said they couldn't see it but everybody went to look for it.

F:	How can you look for something you couldn't see?
Ella:	It was too deep down. We just couldn't see it
Millie:	You should have lifted the blanket up for us
F:	Oh look, there he is. I've found him (*I hold him in my hand*) Can you all see him now?
Kelsey:	(*reaches out to stroke him*) I can feel him but not see him
Tyler:	Yeah, oh, I don't know where he is
Lexie:	He might have hopped off again
Millie:	No, he's not there anymore

Interestingly Millie was one of the children who claimed previously to have seen him. I wanted to test her indecision again.

F:	Do you want to hold him Millie?
Millie:	Yes, oh he's so tickly
Poppy (*stroking it*):	We are just stroking our hands. There is nothing there
Ryan:	There is look, tickle tickle
Millie:	But we found different pets
Ryan:	Mrs Stanley's pet hopped away. He might have needed a wee

*Interestingly Poppy, who has imaginary friends, is still finding it difficult to **believe** the pet is **real**.*

Poppy:	Maybe he is just invisible?
Millie:	If he is invisible he must still be in the classroom, maybe in the walls? We might hear him squeaking?

F:	Was my pet an animal then?
Tyler:	He looked like a bird
Jessica:	No, he was a frog that's why he hopped away
Millie:	But frogs don't hop, they jump
Jessica:	He was real because I saw him playing with our toys
Harry:	This is real though *(shows cuddly toy)*
Ella:	It isn't invisible is it
Millie:	We could turn it invisible then he would be real
Ella:	No, he can't move, talk or walk
Millie:	but he was hopping about. How can he hop if he is not real?
Poppy:	I don't think it was real because you didn't buy him from a real pet shop
Harry:	You can't play a game with something that's not real you know

I was interested to see after this dialogue how the children would extend the play as they were obviously puzzled and fascinated by this activity. Had I been lying to them? Why would an adult lie? Or maybe it was real. What was the difference between real and pretend? At the end of the session, I explained to the children that I had indeed been playing a game to help them think about real and pretend.

The children did indeed extend the invisible pet dilemma into their role play; over the course of the week, he had many visits to the vets, escaped several times and was dragged back to the vets. He even visited the Queen, which he obviously enjoyed very much as he was given bones.

Activity: Philosophy club – What is a brain?

I prepared some large sheets of paper and drew an outline of a brain inside a head. I asked the children to fill in with words or images what they felt our brains were, what they contained, how they worked or any other questions or ideas they had about brains. We worked with paints and pens in a circle. The dialogue mostly comprised of us talking informally while creating the paintings. The children engaged with each other throughout the activity. The end section (part 2) of the dialogue was a summing up and shared enquiry about the ideas raised during the painting process.

Lavelle: I've already got a question; does anyone know why brains think?

Madisson: Because the brain thinks and the people say the brain thinks

Buddy: But if our brain can't talk how do we know what to say?

Olivia: There's a brain and like little wires in that what when the brain has thought of something the wires go in your head and tell you what to think

Abbie: One side of our brain helps us to think and learn and the other side tells us the maths questions. I think we have a part that does remembering too

Abbie: We have a part that is like a diary, and what's going to happen next, like a memory box

Tilly: I think our brains have bits that keep all the things we dream of and an empty space for things you haven't dreamed about yet

George: My brain is thinking about what I am doing now, like painting and words

Henry: Mine is thinking of questions

Abbie: This part of my brain is to do with fear
I think there is a part of the brain for things you are scared of

F: Does our brain feel things?

Buddy: It's a part that makes you feel a bit funny like someone's punched you? It's bad like when people go off; you feel that in your tummy and your brain

Freya: When I am tired it's my brain telling me to go to sleep

Tilly: I think it's your legs if they are tired then that goes up your body and spread about in your body bit and that gets tired then that goes up into your head and then it knows you're tired

Abbie: Your brain gets tired and tells your feet

Olivia:	My brain tells me I'm cross or if I'm happy
Abbie:	I've written 'your brain is in charge'
Olivia:	This brain is asleep
Lavelle:	Our brains don't ever even go to sleep do they? Even when we are asleep they are still working
Buddy:	They are trying to get more energy and they are giving you dreams at the same time
Tilly:	I normally dream about scary things

Activities

Am I real?

A life-size paper person

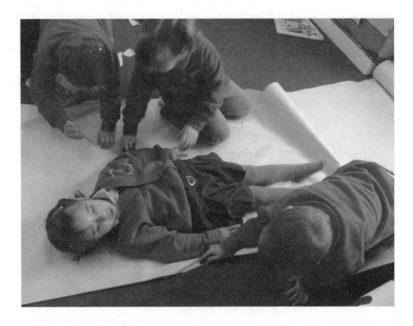

Resources: Large sheet/roll of paper and pens

Year group: Nursery/reception/early enquiries. Ages 3–8 years.

Skill focus: First thoughts. Clarifying ideas.

Thinking focus: What is a person? What makes something real?

Presentation: Roll out a large sheet of paper and ask for a volunteer to lay down on the paper. Ask another child to draw around that person. Return volunteers to the circle.

Conversation and thinking time

Ask the children to think silently for 1 minute about whether they think this is a real person?

Ask children to share their thoughts about this question.

Can they prove whether their ideas are correct?

Introduce the question: 'What can this real person do?'

Watch together to see if it can do the suggested things. If not can the children explain why not?

Introduce the question: 'Can we make it real? If so, how?'

The children might discuss using magic; if this is the case, try getting them to do some spells and ask why they haven't worked.

If the children say it is not real because it has no face, get someone to add the details to see if this works. Again, if not, why not?

Last words

Ask the children if they can explain what the differences are between the drawn round figure and the actual person who was drawn round. Can they give further examples of things that are not real?

Questions for the facilitator to reflect on

- Were all children able to participate and contribute their ideas and suggestions?
- Were children able to think about the differences between real and not real?
- Were the class able to say whether they have a collective answer to the original question?

Be my friend

Stimulus: A talking computer

Year group: Nursery/reception/early enquiries – ages 3–8 years

Skill focus: Making distinctions. Identifying human characteristics. Rethinking initial ideas

Thinking focus: What is a friend? What is thinking? Can a computer think?

Preparation: Write a document using Word on the computer saying, 'I want to be your friend. Will you play with me?'

Presentation: Open the Word document and explain that the computer would like to talk to the children. Select the text and press windows and 'S' button simultaneously. The computer should now speak the two sentences. (Mac users should select apple & S).

Conversation and thinking time

Ask the children to discuss in pairs what their answer to the computer will be.

First words

Bring the children back to the circle and ask them to show their decisions using voting cards or 'stand up/sit down' voting. Ask those children who said yes to explain what they will do with the computer to be 'friends'?

Building

Encourage all children to think critically about whether the computer really will be able to participate in the activities suggested. What couldn't it do? Would the computer need to be able to think in order to be a friend?

Last words

Was the computer really talking?

What is different about the way humans think and the way a computer 'thinks'? What is thinking?

Ask the children to vote again on the same question. Has anyone changed his or her mind? If so, can they explain why?

Follow-up thinking

Ask the children to think about or design a computer that could be a friend. What would it need to do to be a friend? Would this be, effectively, a robot?

Follow this session up with a session on robots to further explore artificial intelligence and concepts that may have arisen from this session.

Questions for the facilitator to reflect on

- Were the children able to think critically about the capabilities and deficiencies of a computer?
- Did they build upon the idea that a friend would need to be able to think independently to be able to communicate?
- Did they show understanding of human emotions?
- Did the children disagree using facts or evidence?
- Did the children show evidence that their thinking had moved on? Could they recognize a change in thinking?

The book of good and bad

Stimulus: Set of fairy tale character cards or figures.

Stimulus details: Set of figures, toys, puppets or pictures depicting a dragon, king, evil queen, Big Bad Wolf, witch, an ogre, prince, knight etc.

Year group: Nursery/reception/early enquiries – ages 3–8 years.

Skill focus: Justifying a choice. Agreeing and disagreeing with other choices. Introducing bigger concepts.

Thinking focus: Thinking about how characters behave and why. Understanding the bigger concepts that underlie the general ideas of 'good' and 'bad'.

Preparation

Make sure children are familiar with the fairy tales through story and role-play experiences.

Prepare two books by folding a large sheet of paper in half. Write 'big book of good' on the cover page of one and 'big book of bad' on the cover of the other.

Provide small pieces of paper for children to draw on. You will also need glue and pens.

Presentation

Introduce the characters and explain that the children will be helping to make two books about good and bad characters.

Conversation and thinking time

Allow thinking and talking time in pairs or small groups. Ask the children to tell each other everything they know or think about the characters, deciding whether they think they are good or bad. Ask children to draw and name the characters if appropriate.

Thinking together activity

Bring the class back to the circle. Ask the children one at a time to place their drawing or character (card or figure) inside their chosen book giving their reasons why.

Allow all the children to contribute and encourage children to say whether they agree or disagree with the book chosen. The drawings can then be stuck in the books or a representation of the figure drawn by the Teacher.

Building

Ask the children to say what it is that they think makes the characters either good or bad (some may be both!) write these down as concepts such as jealousy, anger, magic, appearance and so on, in the book next to the drawings.

Last words

Ask the children to review which big concepts are to do with 'badness' and which with 'goodness'

Follow-up thinking

Allow the children to play with and sort figures or cards into good and bad groups. Display the finished books in the book area for the children to share and talk about.

Questions for facilitator to reflect on

- Did the children focus on behaviours of characters?
- Could they explain why the behaviour could be seen as good or bad?
- Could the children see where there were agreement and disagreement about behaviours of character?
- Were you able to introduce understanding of bigger concepts effectively?

Cages

Stimulus: Pictures from two Anthony Browne books – one showing an Orangutan in his enclosure in the zoo and one showing Hansel in the witch's cage.

Stimulus details: Page 22 of *Hansel & Gretel* by Anthony Browne and page 19 from *Zoo* by Anthony Browne.

Year group: Reception/Key Stages 1 and 2 – ages 5–11 years.

Skill focus: To look for similarities and comparisons between two pictures.

Thinking focus: To use empathy to consider human and animal rights.

Preparation

Allow the children time to play with zoos. Talk about experiences of visits to the zoo, share photographs and look at a range of information and storybooks about zoos and wild animals.

Presentation

Show the children the two illustrations from the book without the stories. Ask the children to look for things that are the same or different in the pictures. You may need to provide clarification that the orangutan is in a zoo enclosure.

Conversation and thinking time

Allow the children to look closely at the two pictures asking them to compare similarities or differences. Allow the children to discuss their ideas in partners/small groups. Reception children may wish to draw their thoughts and ask adults to scribe their words.

Question making/airing

Bring children back to the circle and ask them to share a question or statement/observation about the pictures. Record these thoughts on a large sheet of paper.

Question/theme choosing

Ask whether anyone can offer a question that would sum up what ideas have been most keenly talked about so far. For less experienced children, ask for a statement and model how to turn it into a question or questions.

First words

Ask children to discuss the question in pairs or small groups first and then share their thoughts with the class.

Building

Ask children to put themselves into the position of the characters in the pictures. Encourage discussion about these feelings and reasons they might feel this way.

Last words

Revisit the original question. Ask children to show whether they have reached a decision using voting cards. (Double-sided cards with 'agree/disagree' symbols) or by standing up to agree and remain seated to disagree.

Follow-up thinking

Prepare a question or next question from the dialogue to send home in philosophy journal if used. And/or allow children opportunities to build/design/draw zoos for people. What would humans need in their cages to make them happy? Allow them to also redesign zoos for animals.

Questions for facilitator to reflect on

- Were the children able to see any similarities such as the orange peel on the floor?
- Could they comment on differences such as size and appearance of enclosures?
- Were they able to put themselves in the position of the trapped characters and show empathy?
- Could they give reasons why the characters are in enclosures?
- Could they see inequality or injustice?
- Were children able to make a decision and vote on the final question?

Monster at school

Stimulus: Large drawing of a monster.

Stimulus details: Draw a monster with a closed mouth (no teeth), three arms, four legs and a tail. Ensure that it looks neither friendly nor frightening.

Year group: Nursery/reception – ages 3–5 years

Skill focus: Sharing ideas. Listening as part of a group. Making a decision. Revisiting a question after dialogue.

Thinking focus: Should we judge from appearance only?

Presentation

Explain to the children that you have a difficult decision to make. You met a monster on the way home last night and he asked if he could come to school tomorrow?

Making a decision

Ask the children to vote on their answer to this question using double-sided voting cards or with a 'stand up/sit down' vote.

Conversation and thinking time

Ask those children who voted yes to form a group and the children who voted no to form another group. Allow the children a few minutes to share their reasons within the groups.

First words

Bring the groups back to the circle. Ask the children with the majority vote to share their reasons. Encourage the children from both groups to give their reasons.

What would be the good things and the bad things about having a monster at school?

Building

Introduce further facts about the monster to see if it changes thinking. For example, what if this monster smelt really bad? What if the monster was so small he could fit into a pocket? What if this monster was really clever?

Last words

Review the main ideas put forward and then revisit the original question. Ask the children to show their answers using voting cards. (Double-sided cards with agree/disagree symbols) or by standing up to agree and remain seated to disagree.

Have any children changed their answers. If so, ask them if they can say why.

Questions for facilitator to reflect on

- Were children able to make a decision and vote on the first and final question?
- Could they recognize when their thinking changed in response to different scenarios?
- Did all children get a chance to speak both in the smaller groups and the larger community?
- Were you able to introduce scenarios that might enable children to see from a different perspective?

Perfect people

Stimulus: Playdough people and letter from Planet Leader.
Stimulus details: Letter from the Planet Leader. This letter is also online for you to print off.

> *Dear people,*
>
> *I am giving you a very important job. I am going on holiday and need you to carry on my work. You must create some people for my new planet but they must be the very best people in every way.*

Please let me know all about the people you make for me. I have given you some people making material. Please create carefully. We cannot risk any mistakes.

Thank you
Leader Xon of Planet Plato.

Year group: Nursery/reception/Key Stage 1 – ages 3–7 years
Skill focus: First thoughts. Clarifying ideas.
Thinking focus: What is a person?

Preparation
Allow time for children to explore books and stories about a variety of people.

Presentation
This activity is best done in smaller groups of five or six children at a time, working around a table. Prepare enough playdough for each child to form a model person (you may wish to provide different colours). Read the stimulus letter to them and ask them if they can make the perfect person. Join in this activity yourself.

Conversation and thinking time
While the children create their 'people', they chat informally about what they are doing to make their person. What does it need to look like? What colour have they chosen?

First words
As the models progress, ask the children questions such as would it matter if your person had no arms? Eyes? Heart? Legs? Etc.

Allow them to express their ideas about what makes a perfectly functioning person.

Building
Introduce the idea that the person you have made might not be accepted by the leader because it is sometimes badly behaved. Can they suggest some things that it does wrong?

Ask the children if they can help you 'fix' your person so that it is perfect again?

Last words

Do the children think there can ever be the perfect person or is it alright if they make mistakes or look different?

Questions for facilitator to reflect on

- Were all children able to participate and contribute their ideas and suggestions?
- Were children able to discuss whether physical difference makes a person incomplete or not?
- Were they able to develop thinking to think about behaviour?

Royal invitations

Stimulus: Fairy tale characters/cards and large paper/pens.

Stimulus details: Prepare an invitation from the 'King' requesting help from the children to decide which characters should be invited to the Royal Party and why.

Year group: Nursery/reception/Key Stage 1 – ages 3–8 years

Skill focus: Making a decision and justifying it. Persuasive argument. Working as a community to reach agreement. Listening to others. Sensitivity to disagreement.

Thinking focus: Identifying behaviours of fairy tale characters. Thinking about what constitutes good behaviour. Caring thinking.

Preparation

Ensure children are familiar with fairy tales. Allow opportunities for role play and hotseating as fairy tale characters.

Presentation

Read the letter asking the children to help. Enlist the children's help to take out the figures/cards from a bag one at a time and talk together about who/what the characters are. Allocate each child with a figure/card of his or her choice. Explain that the children will be speaking on behalf of their characters to give a reason why they should be allowed to attend the Royal Party.

Conversation and thinking time

Ask children to look carefully at the collection of figures/cards and discuss in pairs or small groups their first thoughts on the behaviours of each other's characters.

First words

Ask volunteers to ask someone to explain why their character should be allowed to attend the party.

Building

Encourage the class to help each other find reasons why characters should be allowed to attend. Encourage children to wonder if there are reasons why characters might have behaved badly? For example, is the wolf really bad if he only ate the pig because he was starving? Dragons know they are scary and can they help it? Can witches still do bad spells if they leave their wands at home? Was the Giant right to have been cross if Jack had stolen his gold?

Last words

Ask the children which characters they found hardest to allow into the party. Were there any that they felt really were not good enough to come?

Questions for facilitator to reflect on

- Could the children treat each other with respect?
- Did they try and help each other find reasons?
- Did they listen carefully to each other?
- Could they begin to empathize with characters?

Reflective questions about early enquiries

- What skills do you notice the children bring to these enquiries?
- In which way does adult facilitation move thinking on?
- How can you use the children's interests to create opportunities for enquiry?
- What are the differences between scientific and philosophical enquiries?
- What next steps will you need to take in order to make these early enquiries become more philosophical?

6

Think Again – Better Thinking

Checking thinking for accuracy

When children start to participate in enquiries, we often take it for granted that when we ask them to make a choice, they understand what they are doing and why. This is why the question board is so vital in the early days of P4C.

It is, however, even more important in a shared enquiry that their thinking becomes visible. If the children have made no effort at responsible choosing, then the rest of the group cannot access and use this invisible thinking to move the enquiry forward.

Up to this point in the child's philosophical development, we have been developing the building blocks of dialogue. What must happen next is to do with rigour and consequence of visible philosophical thought. This happens because we as facilitators will demand it. We must not be content to allow inconsistent thinking without accountability because this is not philosophy. The following activities will support this development of rigour. Many of these activities could be used in the same way as the earlier question board activities but will also benefit from more lengthy explorations.

The following activities are designed to become increasingly challenging, from the early stages of taking ownership and responsibility of choice to the ethical implications of their statements and ideas.

Activity: Responsibility of choice

This activity involves the use of choosing cards. These are double-sided cards with a smiley face on one side and a sad face on the other. I keep one for each child in my philosophy toolbox. This toolbox also contains concept cards and skills cards, A5 paper and pens.

In addition to these specific skill training activities, I also use the cards to illustrate 'wonky thinking' in an enquiry. Most children move on from needing the cards and quickly learn that they have to remember their choice and give a reason for it. Children also quickly recognize through using this visual aid to a choice when others are giving answers that are inconsistent with the card they are showing. In this situation, we as facilitators can praise this recognition and model the language required for consistent thinking.

How to facilitate an enquiry using Choice cards

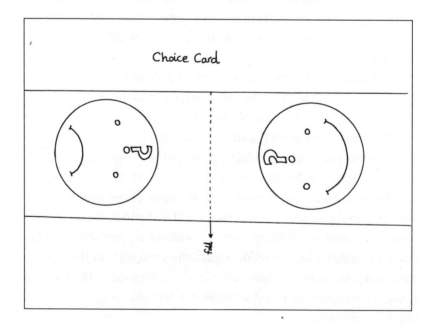

Choice Card

Activities for developing consistent thinking

For the following activities, arrange the group into a thinking circle. Allocate a choosing card to each child. Explain that the red question mark means a negative choice – for example, 'no', 'bad', 'disagree'. The green side indicates a positive answer – for example, 'yes', 'good' or 'agree'. Explain that you will read out the following statements and that they must not use their voices but instead think carefully and show their answer by displaying the appropriate coloured question mark flat down on the floor. Reassure the children that we are not necessarily looking for a correct answer but one that is consistent with their reasoning.

Activity: Do I think what I think I think?

Start with a few statements that the children will know that there is a correct answer to such as:

The sun is hot
Babies hatch out of eggs
Snow is cold
We live on the moon
Apples grow on trees
We eat mud for breakfast
Cars have wheels
I had toast for breakfast
I have a pet
I have a birthday in September
Tigers go to school

Ask the children to display their answer card face down showing their chosen colour. This will get them familiar with understanding which colour means yes and which means no.

Now deliver some of the following statements to indicate that people think different things. You may wish to record how many red cards and how many green cards are shown for each statement. This will ensure the children are matching the colours with the positive or negative word. Vary the way you present the statements to ensure children understand the language of agreement and disagreement.

Would it be 'good' (*green card*) or 'bad' (*red card*) if . . .
Do you think 'yes' (*green card*) or 'no' (*red card*)?
Do you 'agree that' (*green card*) or 'disagree that' (*red card*) . . .
Some statements:

Brussels sprouts are delicious
Spiders are cute
Chocolate makes people happy
Pink is my favourite colour
Roller coasters are fun

Activity: Understanding negative statements

This is often an area where children experience confusion. Encouraging children to use choosing cards to explore when a statement may be incorrect will enable them to develop an ear for inconsistency in thinking. This can be a multistage thinking process because we are asking them to identify: a) what is x? and b) is x actually X?

Some statements:

Fairies are not big
Hot porridge isn't cold
Old things are not new
Dogs do not bark
Airplanes do not have wings
Dragons do not breathe fire
Elephants do not have trunks

Logic and reasoning

Activity: Alternative thinking exercises

This set of questions is designed to encourage children to think creatively about the positive or negative consequences of an idea. There are often many reasons why people make decisions in their lives. The choices we make are not always simple to explain or to make judgements about or indeed they may not even be 'conscious' decisions.

However, life is a continuous succession of choices that we have to make based on our own moral codes or the ethical codes of the society we live in. It is important that the children understand why they think what they think. We might call it 'transparent thinking' where an end position is held through a series of conscious decisions.

Allowing children to consciously explore their reasoning enables them to think about the many shades of grey thinking that lie behind our social and moral obligations and conscience that is attached to them.

This is an extension to the 'Would You Dare?' activities where two sides of an idea are presented. The skill behind this exercise is to develop an understanding of the thought process rather than the enquiry process. We cannot form our own opinions readily until we have an understanding of the logical arguments of the opposition.

The children could work in pairs or small groups to create their own scenarios, which can then be bought back into the enquiry circle with the whole group.

Example
Under what circumstances would it be acceptable to bring a dinosaur back to life?

If it was the size of a hamster and had no teeth?
If it could tell us how the earth began?
If it's living DNA held the cure for cancer?

Further thinking challenges to present
Under what circumstances would it be acceptable to . . .?

Destroy the last flower on earth?
Break into someone's home and eat their porridge?
Harm another living thing?
Tell someone a lie?
Lay down in the supermarket and scream and kick?
Put a sign around your neck saying 'go away!'?
Lock your best friend up in jail?
Steal the most valuable diamond in the world?
Cheat in a game of football?
Eat your dearest pet?
Pretend to be someone else?

Activity: Good news bad news

The aim of this activity is to challenge children to think of an alternative viewpoint in response to a statement. The opposing 'good news/bad news' format can be played either as a game where everyone takes part by travelling around the circle or as a 'find a space to talk' exercise.

The following statements will start off the activity but encouraging the children to create their own will also be a valuable exercise as they will have to use their alternative thinking skills to create these.

Nominate somebody to choose either a good news or bad news statement from the list below. Challenge the group to keep the thread of related good news/bad news answers going for as long as possible.

Example

Good news – I have found a magic wand
Bad news – it belongs to an evil witch
Good news – I have used the wand to make myself invisible
Bad news – she can still smell you with her super sensitive magic nose
Good news – I am having kippers for tea and they will disguise the smell
Bad news – the kippers are poisoned
Good news – I will be able to magic myself better with the wand.

See how long the children can keep this going.

Good news suggestions

The Queen is coming for tea
I have won the lottery
My dad is buying me a present
My cat is pregnant
My grandparents are coming to visit
The weather will be getting warmer
Food prices are at an all time low

Bad news suggestions

I have an infectious disease
I have lost my phone
I have been evicted from my house

My school burned down
My friend has left the country
My teeth have fallen out
I am allergic to chocolate
I have shrunk to the size of a pepperpot

Activity: Yes but, no but

The following questions may appear at first glance to be closed questions. Any questions we ask require nothing more than a yes or no answer. These tell us little and offer even less in terms of dialogue. This exercise is designed to challenge pupils to think of a response that goes beyond the yes/no limitations.

Method

Ask the children to sit in a circle. Prepare cards or folded paper with the following questions on them. Ask for a volunteer to choose one question at random and read it out. The volunteer can either address the question to a certain member of the group or pupils can find a space to reply if they have a good response. Ensure you clarify which method you wish the children to use first.

Encourage the group to work together supplying alternative answers for as long as possible; if creative ideas run dry, then another question may be drawn. Ask the children to consider which questions were easiest to keep going and which were hardest.

Example

If your fingers were made of chocolate would you eat them?
Yes
No but, you wouldn't be able to hold a pen
Yes but, I could write in chocolate smudges
No but, you might fail your exams
Yes but, I would use a voice recorder
No but, you would feel too sick to talk
Yes but I would never be hungry again

Alternatively, if the answer was 'No', the group would have to find a 'Yes but' to respond with.

'Yes but, No but' questions

> *If your friend had purple spots would you play with him/her?*
> *If your grandparents moved to a haunted house would you still visit them?*
> *If you had supersonic ears would you listen to secrets?*
> *If money grew on trees would you put high fences round them?*
> *If you found a magic wand would you hand it in?*
> *If you discovered an alien would you show it to anyone?*
> *If you grew superfast robot legs would you enter every race?*
> *If spiders could talk would you squash them?*
> *If you saw your brother steal would you tell?*
> *If you had someone else's brain would you become them?*
> *If your favourite bedtime teddy was worth a million pounds would you sell it?*
> *If everyone could hear your thoughts would you think differently?*
> *If there was no money, would you still want to be rich?*
> *If you had automatic goal scoring football boots would you wear them?*
> *If you had wings would you ever use your legs?*

 ## Activity: True or false

> A robot is metal – All metal things are robots
> I like all vegetables – I like broccoli
> All animals have four legs – Kangaroos have four legs
> Smiling means you are good – Smiling baddies are good
> All food is good for us – Sweets are good for us
> We must share everything – I will share my mum
> All magic is good – All witches are good
> Everything is real – Monsters are real
> We are all the same – We all have blonde hair
> All people are nice – Robbers are nice
> All furry animals are cuddly – Fierce lions are cuddly
> All cars go fast – Broken cars go fast

Children taking control of thinking

As children become more confident in the rigour of P4C, we must prepare to hand over this rigorous facilitation to them. We will have taught by this time that 'wonky' or careless thinking will not be tolerated. Children will understand that, in the same way that we do not accept incorrect answers in other curriculum areas, we do not have to accept indecisive or incorrect methods of thinking in philosophy. We want our children to be comfortable in a community of enquiry where trust and honesty are commonplace, where the group has a commitment to respectful yet challenging thinking. Children should understand that in philosophy we must hold no prisoners because we are trying to work together to further the cause in a quest for common understanding and acceptance. Opinion is determined by feelings not intellect but we have to move from emotional to reasoned decisions in order to work together in an environment of collective responsibility.

One way of developing this rigour is to entrust the children with the task of challenging the statements rather than attacking the thinker. The following exercise will develop a spirit of collective reasoned discussion where persuasive argument relies on working as a team.

Activity: Duelling with thoughts

Divide the group into two and give each group one of the two thinking scenarios from each exercise. Allow the groups time to discuss their thoughts on their given scenario. Explain that while they might not necessarily believe the statement, they should try and think of as many persuasive arguments for that case as possible. Bring the two groups back together and challenge them to present their reasoning. They should aim to challenge the oppositional viewpoints attacking the thinking not the person.

Some examples

Which should we have?

> *School with no fun or fun with no school?*
> *Would it be better to turn water into gold or gold into water?*
> *Sweets and no money or money and no sweets?*
> *Books but no ability to read or ability to read with no books?*
> *Happiness and no friends or friends and no happiness?*
> *Music and no voice or voice and no music?*

Sun and no holidays or holidays and no sun?
Cars and no petrol or petrol and no cars?
Flowers and no rain or rain and no flowers?
Beauty and no love or love and no beauty?

Advanced thinking: Working with ethical problems

Activity: The problematic hamster

You will need the three scenario cards labelled 1, 2 and 3 to be read out in that order.

Read out the scenario 1 and ask children to decide on their choice, thinking about whether their decision could be judged morally right or wrong.

Ask them to draw their choices and to compare the decisions made. Are they the same as those of others in the group? Where and how do they differ? Discuss this as a group. Is anyone right or wrong? Can there be a card in between right or wrong?

As we feed in more information, ask the children whether they have changed their thinking, does it become easier or harder to make a morally correct decision?

 Scenario 1

Your friend goes on holiday and asks you to look after her hamster.

When she gets back, she comes round to ask for it back. But you have grown to love him. What is the morally correct thing to do?

- Convince your friend you still need the hamster
- Make excuses so you can keep him as long as you can
- Return him straight away
- Refuse to give him back.

Scenario 2

Just before your friend returns from holiday, you find evidence that she has joined the hamster racing club which is run in a very cruel way. What should you do now?

- Keep the hamster to prevent it being hurt
- Return the hamster
- Promise to return the hamster only if she promises to leave the racing club.

Scenario 3

Your friend attacks you or the hamster in order to get it back. What do you do?

- Set the hamster free to protect it
- Hit back
- Get the anti-hamster racing society to come and help you
- Return the hamster.

Think about ...

Are you a fair and just person? Do you consider yourself a fair and just person? Is this important? What does this mean?

Plato said that to be 'just is to be fair'. Do you agree? What about after you have thought through the hamster dilemma?

Can we act unjustly to do something good?

Who should we be fair to?

Should we be fair to our friends? Our enemies?

Can we be just to ourselves?

Can we be unjust to ourselves?

Can we be just if we do not know ourselves?

What do we need to know about ourselves in order to know ourselves?

Follow-up

Try to write a letter to the friend in the dilemma explaining your choices.

Reflective questions on better thinking

- What makes an enquiry more than a conversation?
- How can children demonstrate intellectual rigour?
- How can we hand over responsibility for whole class thinking to the children?

- How can we model rigour in our teaching?
- What are the consequences of lazy thinking?
- What is the difference between thinking and rigorous thinking?
- Does thinking about thinking influence change?
- How do you know that your children understand the consequences of their thinking?

7

Continuing the Philosophical Journey

What does the traditional P4C enquiry look like?

Philosophy in the classroom can take many forms – from the early days of presenting questions to introducing philosophical skills, to encouraging philosophical play and storytelling and finally to the point where the children have acquired the skills needed for reasonable and reasoned enquiry. So far, this manual has concentrated on the development of philosophical skills. In order to reach the point where children become facilitators of thinking, we must first consider the journey.

The structure of a traditional P4C session

The structure of the session will involve the following elements.

> **Stimulus:** The starting point of the session. Something that gets you and the children thinking.

Thinking time: The children have some time to think, draw, write and finally produce questions about the stimulus. There are periods of quietness and time to talk to peers and adults such as the class teacher, LSA and visitors.

Conceptual analysis: The children explore their initial ideas and questions through analysis of concepts that they feel match their thoughts.

Questions: The children are encouraged to present their constructed questions. The questions are collected, connected and analysed using a range of strategies.

Dialogue: The children build their argument through reasoning, explaining, agreeing and disagreeing. The facilitator will use questioning to bring out the philosophical dimension.

Closure: The facilitator uses a range of strategies to close a session, for example, summing up, finding the next question, asking for comments.

Evaluation: Using the assessment building blocks. Talking together as a class to discuss feelings about the session, which skills were used and which need to be developed. The main thing to remember is that as long as you stick to the principle that the children lead the discussion and try to uncover the philosophical, you will develop your own style that works for you and the children.

Starting the session

Practicalities

To start the session, the children need to be seated in a circle. This enables all the children to see each other and be able to direct their comments anywhere within the circle. You may wish to experiment with ways of sitting. You may wish children to sit on the carpet, bring chairs or stools to the area or move desks into a circle. If you have a large class and intend to use journals or paper for thinking time, you could allow a group to do their drawing at the table and return to the circle for collection of questions. An ideal number for a community of enquiry is between 12 and 24 but I have worked with up to 30 children. The difficulty with large groups is ensuring that all children get a chance to speak and time taken to collect in questions; however, solutions to these difficulties are offered later in the section. Conversely, working with too small a group could mean that the children are more self-conscious or are unable to offer a wide enough range of ideas to build upon effectively.

The stimulus

This could be any of the following:

- Question board activities
- Thinking exercises or questions offered in this manual
- Picture book, poem, short story, extract from a novel or picture book
- Media/social media extract
- Historical artefact
- Photograph/illustration/painting/work of art
- Piece of music/musical lyrics
- Newspaper/magazine article/comics.

Any stimulus used needs to get the children and facilitator wondering. The best stimuli will provide a higher level of ambiguity. This ambiguity is necessary to allow the children to produce a wide range and depth of ideas and questions. The most fertile starting points are those that do not present one theme or moral but contain strong elements of puzzlement and allow the children to engage their own emotions. The stimulus should be open ended enough so that the children can recognize the philosophical concepts within it and can ask questions that cannot be answered by the text or illustration alone. The stimulus must provoke a reaction from the children that can be explored. Ideas, concepts and theories can be tested out among the peer group and the children can feel safe in the knowledge that there are no absolute right or wrong answers. The best stimuli are those that excite and engage the children's imaginations. The discussion will flow more easily about a question raised from a stimulus that the child is able to relate to. They will be more able to put themselves in a position of empathy. We should aim to provoke a curious and engaged response as the quest for truth will be based on deeper thinking about issues that are relevant and important to their own lives, culture, experience and aspirations.

A stimulus can be chosen to fit in with a current topic or scheme but you should always be prepared for it not to journey in your expected direction. This is because, ultimately, it is the children's enquiry and they lead the direction of the dialogue. As a skilled facilitator, you will aim to develop their thinking towards the philosophical but it will ultimately be the concept *they* are interested in discussing that will be the most fertile ground.

Thinking time for younger/less experienced children

After the stimulus has been shared, invite the children to spend some time thinking about puzzling or interesting things that it has evoked. The pupils are encouraged to talk about the stimulus quietly in small groups. In the Early Years classroom, it is useful to make use of additional adult support to facilitate and focus language within these small groups, ensuring that children understand the task and get a chance to talk and listen to each other. They should be encouraged to discuss and share thoughts and ideas about strange or interesting parts of the stimulus. It is helpful for the children to be given a large paper to work on during this process. Encourage the children in the groups to work collaboratively to draw these ideas and thoughts.

You may find it useful to write down key ideas or questions that arise during this process.

This shared thinking time is good preparation for future enquiries where you may wish the children to use their journals to develop personal thoughts, ideas and questions. When the children have had a few minutes to do this, bring them back into the circle and ask them to review their ideas. In the early days of enquiry, the questions may have to be raised and modelled by the adult facilitator(s). The facilitator should use interesting statements offered by the children to develop the thinking. For example, if a child has offered an opinion such as 'girls don't like football', then you will need to develop thinking through a line of questioning such as: Is that always true? Do any girls here like football? Do you think girls and boys are different? If so, in which ways? Is this because we are told what to like? If you swapped brains with a boy would you like football then?

This overt modelling of questions enables the children to very quickly understand the purpose of philosophical thinking. It is this questioning that engages the children in purposeful dialogue. The facilitator must develop a disciplined approach to modelling the talking and listening processes, ensuring the children take turns to speak and do not digress from the ideas in development (*see the role of the facilitator*).

Early enquiries will involve more movement and use of props and resources. The facilitator may also find it useful to record ideas pictorially on large sheets of paper that the children can engage with.

Thinking time for older/more experienced philosophical thinkers

After the stimulus has been shared, invite the children to talk quietly with partners or in small groups about the stimulus. Encourage them to discuss strange or interesting parts of the story or tell each other their thoughts. After a few minutes, ask the children to close their eyes or sit silently for a few minutes to give them time to reflect on their thoughts. When they feel ready, they may begin to draw their ideas and form questions from these thoughts to record in their thinking journal. These individual journals are used by the children to record their thoughts and ideas in whichever format the child prefers. The journals should ideally be A4 sized with blank white pages. It can be used both in class and at home and serves to show ongoing progress and development in the child's philosophical questioning and thinking. Children should be encouraged to jot down any thoughts or questions they have during the dialogue that they wish to raise later or think about in private. They should also be encouraged to draw pictures and mind maps that illustrate their thinking, from which they can draw their ideas and questions. This is especially important for the younger children or those with communication difficulties. The children will find it much easier to talk about their drawing, its significance and relevance to the stimulus. As the children draw their illustrated thoughts, the facilitator is able to move among the group. Some children may need the added reassurance and support of an adult with whom they could share their ideas. The teacher can talk quietly with these children and ask questions about what parts of the stimulus they found interesting, likes or dislikes and gain clarification from the child about the question or statements they offer. This part of thinking time can serve as a form of rehearsal for less confident speakers, enabling them to feel more confident when presenting their questions or ideas later in the session. The teacher may also ask younger or less literate children if they wish to have their questions written in their journal and this can be done during the thinking and drawing time. It is helpful for the adult to scribe the question exactly in the journals.

Older or more experienced pupils are encouraged to think of as many questions as they can and also to make their questions more philosophical.

The class may need around 15 minutes to do this. Children who finish quickly are encouraged to illustrate another thought or question or talk quietly to someone else who has finished his or her work. Remind the children that this is still a thinking time and even when they have finished, they must respect others in the group who are trying to think and work. Enforce the sensible behaviour rules and ask children to ensure they are talking to others about their thoughts and ideas only. The children may also use this time to revisit the stimulus. They may wish to check details of the story or ask for further clarification of the stimulus. This time can also enable the adult to listen to the views of those children who are less likely to contribute to the dialogue later. At relevant times in the discussion, the teacher could bring in that child's ideas, confirming with that child if they have the details correct.

Example

> 'When I was talking with . . . she said something really interesting about . . .'
>
> 'Am I right?'
>
> 'Can you tell us why you think that?'

Some children may well feel more able to speak in front of others when they have received the go-ahead that their idea is considered important. Another way of doing this is to draw other children into the quiet discussions during thinking time. The smaller group setting means children may be less wary of airing their ideas. During the dialogue session, the facilitator can call upon more confident members of those small groups to mention the ideas of others in their group.

Example

> 'When we were talking about this in thinking time . . . said they thought . . .'

This form of peer group recognition could also be a very strong starting point for encouraging a less confident speaker to participate in the session.

Another useful way to encourage children to think and talk before they formulate and present their question is to ask them to move among themselves and compare their illustrated questions. In discussing and talking about what their picture represents, the children will find others who are interested in the same theme or idea as themselves. When the children have found others with a common interest, they can then group together and negotiate a 'shared' question.

Exploring the concepts

Introducing the philosophical concepts at this point allows for better understanding of the purpose of the enquiry. It allows pupils and facilitators alike to make connections between the questions and ideas in the context of philosophical exploration.

From early enquiries with younger or less experienced philosophers, it is important to enable the children to understand that we are not merely having a conversation but plotting a philosophical journey. This journey involves an understanding of what we are talking about and why.

Concept cards can be used from very early on to illustrate visually what the children are exploring. In the early days of enquiry these might consist of a small group of ideas such as 'good', 'bad', 'magic' and 'reality'.

Explaining to the children and showing them a card that depicts the concept will familiarize them not just with what the cards represent but what the concept looks like and feels like in a variety of situations in their own lives and the lives and experiences of others. What is good to one person may be bad to another. What one person may think of as real others might think imaginary. The cards can be shown and explained to the children when the relevant concepts occur in dialogue.

As facilitators, we should overtly teach the children that, philosophically, we are talking and thinking about a philosophical concept. In the same way as we overtly teach that an object with three sides is a triangle, we must be prepared to teach our children to recognize what concepts we are talking about. For example, 'What we are talking about here is something which we call "Reality"'. Once the children have started to understand the meaning of concepts, we can then explore further what these concepts might mean to others and where and why there may be disagreement or agreement.

Concepts with older or more experienced children

Through early exposure and drip feeding of the concepts in early enquiries and philosophical play, children with more experience will be able to recognize the philosophical content of any presented stimulus, but concept cards are still very useful.

After thinking time, it is helpful to present the concept cards one at a time. Ask the children to identify which cards are represented in their thoughts or questions about the stimulus. The facilitator may wish to refer to concepts in their opening comments – 'Was this about Jealousy? Truth? Power?'

The children will be encouraged to look more deeply into the stimulus and its meaning and then relate their own thoughts to a bigger issue. Allowing this time for collaborative and shared understanding of conceptual identity in itself leads to philosophical dialogue, allowing the children to explore different ideas about the meaning of that concept itself.

Questioning

Younger/less experienced children

Before you expect the children to ask philosophical questions, it is necessary to have allowed them to explore modelled questions in a variety of philosophical situations in the classroom. Learning to ask questions that can be used in enquiry is a skill that needs practice. Ensure that children understand the purpose of why they are asking questions. They should understand that questions are challenging and fun. That discovering what they mean is more important than finding an 'answer'. The fact that the questions are seemingly unanswerable is what truly engages, stimulates and motivates. As children become more experienced across the range of philosophical skills, the questions will become a natural part of their enquiry process. It is imperative that in the early stages, adults model how to turn statements into questions; taking time together to ensure they truly understand the meaning behind the statements and not assuming they absolutely know what the child is asking. Take time to engage with statements the children make, allowing time for them to explain their thought processes. If this time for understanding is not given, then the danger is that the questions could become those of the facilitator and not of the child.

When children learn to ask questions in philosophy, they are asking questions about things to which they do not know the answer. They are also asking questions which the facilitator has no answer to either and this can be incredibly empowering to them. The children are encouraged to try and work answers out together within the community of enquiry. It is the quest for the answers that reveals so much; the journey is so adventurous that the children will want to step on many more paths of enquiry. The questions children ask are based on hearing and voicing opinions rather than facts and it is this that enables them in time to learn to trust their own judgements and value their opinions and those of others.

Older/more experienced children

Questions recorded on paper and in the journals should now be looked at again. What concepts do they represent? The questions at this point should now have a clearer philosophical meaning to the community. More experienced children may now see that the wording of their questions could be adjusted for more philosophical clarity.

For example, a factual question such as 'Why did the King go and fight the dragon?' might, after thinking about power, responsibility and war, become 'Is it ok to fight to protect those you love?'

The next stage is to collect all the children's questions in and record them. These questions should be written in the child's exact words with the child's name or initials next to it. It is best to do this on a large piece of paper. There are many ways of managing this process. Collecting all the questions can be quite time consuming but there are ways of speeding this up.

Ways to collect in the questions

One way is to ask the children to volunteer their questions one at a time while the teacher writes them on the paper.

Another method is to use a question hotspot. This could be a circular disc of red paper. The children are allowed to come and stand on the hotspot to present their question. The children are reminded that they can only approach the spot if it is vacant and it serves as a good reminder of the turn-taking ethos that permeates the enquiry. Another advantage of a well-managed hotspot is that other members of the class can be encouraged to join the questioner on the spot if they feel they have the same question. In this case, you must ensure that the wording is exactly the same as the children may not have learnt yet that one word in the question could change its meaning completely.

For example, the question 'Why do people fight each other?' is completely different from 'How do people fight each other?'

More literate children can start to write their questions up on the big paper during thinking time.

They could also record their questions on a post-it note and stick it on the paper.

Additional supporting adults in the classroom could also write up questions from journals on to the big sheet during thinking time.

Shared questions. This method cuts down the number of questions collected in and helps the children see connections between questions. Ask the children to move among the group to find people with a similar question or picture to their own. When they have done this, they can talk to each other about the meanings of their questions or pictures and negotiate between themselves a new question that sums up the group's questions. When this question is presented, the facilitator can put the names of that group with that question.

Paired questions. Ask the children to work in pairs. They should first discuss their thoughts on the stimulus and then work together to negotiate a question. Up to this point, those who are beginning with P4C would have been concentrating on getting the children to develop questioning skills, for example, classify and aim to ask open-ended questions. The next stage is to think about asking questions that can be discussed in a philosophical way. As the children become more familiar with philosophy and have started to make better questions with greater understanding, they will be able to work at a deeper level of thinking with the questions. In addition to explaining the meaning behind their question, they should now be encouraged to think about how their question fits in with those of others and where this questioning will lead to discussion about things that are important to them. When the questions have been collected in, they need to be analysed and clarified. It is through this process that the questions can be fully understood and the children's thinking stimulated.

This can be done by encouraging the children to identify a concept that encapsulates the meaning of the question; again this serves to ensure that the community has a shared understanding of what that question is asking. Philosophy is about challenging assumptions. It is important that we as facilitators do not assume we can understand the child's thinking. It is important that children identify what they want to find out and how to frame their thinking in words that are as clear as possible to others. When the facilitator collects the questions, it is really worth the extra time to ensure that the child has a chance to explain what they are trying to ask and why.

Voting on a question

In the early days of enquiry, it is useful to vote on a question. As you and the children become more confident, you could vote on a concept that has arisen from making links and connections or you may find that the voting process is not even necessary as the children become used to entering the dialogue phase from the clarification of their questions.

Voting on a question can be done in several ways.

Conceptual voting. This allows the children to vote on a concept rather than one individual question. Through analysis of the questions, they could be categorized into concepts. This is particularly helpful when you have lots of questions that are connected to the same question. When the children are able to recognize that a group of questions represents thoughts about say, knowledge or power, they may wish to vote for exploration of what those questions mean within that context. New or secondary questions may arise from voting for a philosophical area of thinking instead of a narrower question directly related to the stimulus.

Uni-voting. Firstly, explain to the children that they are allowed to vote on the questions or concepts exposed through the analysis of questioning. These questions or concepts could be numbered in a random way; the children can choose one question or concept and raise their hands when the one they choose is read out. They must then sit on their hands so they cannot vote again. The facilitator records the number of votes for each question. The one with most votes is the dialogue subject.

Multi-voting. The children may vote as many times as they wish. All votes are counted for each question/concept.

Blind voting. The children vote for one or more questions or concepts but with their eyes closed.

Corner voting. Four questions or concepts are chosen and placed in each corner of the room. The children are reminded where the choices are placed and they must then choose which area to move to.

Ballot voting. Questions or concepts are numbered. The children secretly write down the number and post their votes in a voting bag or box.

Dialogue

The role of the facilitator in a dialogue

The facilitator's job is to ensure that a dialogue is not just a speaking and listening exercise or conversation among children. Allowing a conversation or discussion to just follow its course will not make it a true enquiry. Enquiry comes from the desire to push for deeper understanding. Our ultimate aim as a facilitator is to allow the children to ask and think for themselves. The facilitator must encourage and support the children in their interaction with each other and eventually keep adult involvement to a minimum. This can be achieved relatively quickly when the children understand the importance of the skills involved in enquiry. The children must first understand how to listen, clarify, expand upon and search together for deeper understanding.

The facilitator will initially have to lead the children in a philosophical direction. Below are some useful starting points for the facilitator to use. These questioning skills will help the push for deeper thinking.

Facilitator's questions

- *Can you give me an example of that?*
- *Has that ever happened to you?*
- *Is that always true?*
- *Why do you believe that?*
- *What do you mean by . . .?*
- *Can you say that in a different way?*

- *Is it ever right/OK to . . .?*
- *What is the difference between (a) and (b)?*
- *Is there a difference between (a) and (b)?*
- *Where is that happening?*
- *What is doing the thinking/feeling?*
- *Does anyone agree or disagree with . . .? Why?*
- *Does anyone have a different idea?*
- *How is that connected to . . .?*
- *Whose thoughts are you making links with?*
- *What evidence have you got to back that up?*
- *How could we find that out?*
- *Can you summarize what you have said?*
- *What other reasons would make us believe that?*
- *Would it ever be possible that . . .?*
- *Is that exactly what you meant?*
- *Would there be any circumstances that would make you give a different view?*
- *What might change your mind?*

Children as facilitators

Our ultimate aim is that the children take over the role of facilitator. It is therefore imperative that we give them the language and vocabulary to communicate with each other not just *in* the dialogue but in moving the dialogue further. Overtly teaching phrases to use initially can give the children the confidence to take control of the thinking. Children can be given this control through the ability to recognize when dialogue is off task or contradictory. They should be encouraged to ask for clarification.

The facilitator should initially give the child the exact language to use. For example, 'Say to X – "I don't understand what you mean" or "Can you explain that in a different way?"'

They should be encouraged and given the words to invite others into the dialogue. For example, 'Say to X – "I would like to hear what you think" or "Do you agree or disagree with me?"'

Most importantly, children should be given the powers of facilitation to deal with unwanted and unhelpful behaviours. For example, 'Say to

X – "that behaviour is stopping me from thinking clearly" or "you're not talking about what we are trying to find out."'

With these tools to facilitate, the children will become less reliant on adult facilitation.

Closure and evaluation

Closure is a wrapping up of the session. The children are given a few minutes to quietly reflect on the lesson and the facilitator then asks the children to decide where the dialogue has ended up. What issues have been discussed? Where has there been uncertainty? Where is the focus for further discussion? What question could be chosen or new question negotiated to take home for homework?

Reflecting on the structure of P4C enquiry

- How will you ensure children are enthused by philosophical enquiry?
- How can you record successes and difficulties in your facilitation?
- How can you ensure all children can access the sessions?
- How can you ensure you track the development of pupil's philosophical skills?
- Which stimuli work best with your pupils?
- What do the children see as successes and difficulties of enquiry?
- How can you record pupils' reflections on enquiry?

8
The Final Adventure – Using books for P4C

A hidden world inside the picture book

Ultimately, our journey in philosophical thinking should end up inside a quality picture book. Prior to this, we have encouraged the children to revel in the joy of story through their play and storytelling; now we offer the chance to step into a world where books are appreciated for not just their language and illustration but the messages that lie within. Quality picture books are the ultimate escape and the doorway to deeper thinking about the experiences we dream of, wish for and may have the fortune, or misfortune, of experiencing. The whole of life exists inside books. From the wonder of whether fairies exist to the realism of whether we can ever outrun death, books enable us to connect with our emotions and empathize with others.

Why we use books?

This chapter will look at books that can be used to engage children and young people in philosophical discussion. It will explore the potential for enquiry and offer case studies from children in the Foundation Stage, Key Stage 1 and Key Stage 2 – ages 3–11 years.

Many thanks to the Year 5 pupils from Acle Primary School, Norfolk, facilitated by SAPERE trainer Maria Cornish, of childrenthinking, for providing transcripts of the Key Stage 2 case studies.

The following books have been tried and tested across the Early Years Foundation Stage and into Key Stage 2. Examples of questions that have arisen during enquiry about these books have been included to help practitioners see the possibilities for deep and critical thinking that arise when picture books are used as a stimulus for philosophy.

My top ten recommended books for philosophical enquiry

Introductory picture books that practice early philosophical skills

The following two books introduce younger or inexperienced philosophers to the idea that we can use books to create enquiries. These books form a bridge between early enquiries using play and the more formal enquiry model used when engaging with challenging picture books.

The contents of these early picture books allow a more active and physical exploration of the enquiry skills required for using books for future enquiry.

Would You Rather?

Skills: Making choices and giving reasons, active listening to the ideas of others.

Would you rather? Help a fairy make magic, gnomes dig for treasure, an imp be naughty or Santa Claus deliver presents?

This is an ideal first book for practitioners wishing to discover the potential of introducing philosophical thinking in the classroom. The book presents a variety of scenarios where choices have to be made, but as in the real world, the choices are not always between good and bad but often between bad and bad! Allowing children to explore difficult choices within the safety of this thinking story increases confidence when it comes to transferring this skill to real life. The discovery that others may agree or disagree with your thoughts leads to further discussion about the advantages and disadvantages of the decision-making process.

I am the King

Skills: Decision making, exploration of concepts, challenging assumptions.

What quality makes the best ruler? Strength, fear, cunning, wit or respect?

A crown found on the jungle floor provides an opportunity for the animals of the forest to lay claim to the vacant position of King. Each animal finds a reason for its entitlement to this role but there can only be one crowned sovereign. *I am the King* allows the children to explore and challenge assumptions about the behaviours and appearance of the animals. Exploration of the philosophical concepts behind the nature of Leadership will lead to discussion about fair and just rule for the benefit of the population. What would you do if you were King? What rules would you enforce and why? Why do we need leaders anyway? Could we ever live in a world where everyone was equal?

Community of enquiry

The following picture books can be used as a stimulus for more formal community enquiry.

For each of these books, children will use the skills of active listening, reasoning, agreeing and disagreeing while exploring and deepening their understanding of philosophical concepts.

Tusk Tusk

Concepts: War, peace, differences, tolerance.

What drives people to war? Why do people find it difficult to accept difference? Can we ever live in a world with total acceptance of each other?

Two groups of elephants share the land peacefully with all other creatures but cannot tolerate each other. A war ensues between the two groups and they set about exterminating each other with their elephant trunk guns. Meanwhile, the peace-loving elephants from both sides disappear into the deepest darkest jungle and re-emerge years later as grey elephants. However, the trouble does not stop there. . . .

This book allows children to explore the issues of tolerance, war and peace, and what difference means. Questions may arise that focus on whether there is ever such a thing as a just war? Why is it hard to accept difference? Are some differences harder to accept than others?

Where the Wild Things Are

Concepts: Reality, dreaming, power, responsibility, escape.

This classic picture book is ideal for use when starting enquiries. Max's new world is a place of mysterious curiosity and self-discovery.

His newfound power and responsibility are both liberating and problematic. Children are intrigued by the imagined world where a bedroom can transform into an ocean and where the walls become the world all around. Questions may focus on why Max is chosen as leader? What responsibilities come with his leadership and why does he choose to go home? How does Max's behaviour impact on others in the book? How does imagination work? And can we use imagination to escape from or solve problems?

The Last Noo-Noo

Concepts: Conformity, bullying, making choices.

Marlon has to deal with pressure from both adults and children to relinquish his 'noo-noos' or dummies. Each person in the story has a different perspective on the acceptability of dummies. This leads to exploration of responsibility, growing up and conformity within established social conventions. Marlon shows dogged determination to ignore peer pressure and bullying and finds inventive ways to retain control of his habit. The book allows children to look at the roles of both adults and children in the context of power over others versus the powerfulness of making their own decisions. Who decides what we should do and when? How and why do values and behaviours of a society change? Who is responsible for the behaviour of children and what would happen if there were no adults to decide what children should do?

Edwina the Dinosaur Who Didn't Know She Was Extinct

Concepts: Truth, knowledge, scientific evidence, belief, happiness, acceptance.

Edwina lives in a community where she is welcomed without question. She bakes cookies and helps old ladies cross the road. But Reginald Von Hoobie-Doobie makes it his mission to convince the townspeople that he is right and 'dinosaurs are extinct'. However, Edwina is, in fact, the only one prepared to listen to his case.

This book explores why people believe what they believe. What is the difference between belief and truth? How do we know dinosaurs are actually extinct? What is acceptable evidence of something we may not have seen ourselves? Can we be happy not knowing the truth? In what circumstances would we need actual proof? And does proof always have to be scientific?

The following picture books are recommended for older children or those who have had more experience in philosophy.

Zoo

Concepts: Freedom, captivity, animal rights.

Anthony Browne initially received some criticism about this powerful picture book. It was perceived as anti-zoo propaganda by some reviewers who thought that the message was purely that zoos are wrong. However, this book was designed to encourage thinking about the nature of animals and people. Do the characters in the book mirror the animals or is it the other way round? It will of course raise questioning and discussion about the nature and purpose of zoos. But through exploration of similarities of humans and animals, the children may discuss both human and animal rights. Why for example do we imprison people? Why are some humans more dangerous than others? Do some humans need protection, if so from what or who? Do these issues apply to animals in the same way that we think they do to people?

The Three Robbers

Concepts: Violence, theft, equality, humanity.

This highly successful and widely translated story has been reissued much to the relief of those practicing P4C. The menacing gang of armed robbers are used to a life of pillaging and inducing terror for the sake of acquiring wealth. The puzzlement of the story is that it takes a newly acquired chattel in the form of orphan Tiffany to point out the futility of robbing for money that they do not use! The robbers then use their ill-gotten gains to build a town and community where unloved and orphaned children can grow up happily. The book is disturbing in many ways. The robbers and the children are all in uniform and there is no indication that the robbers are remorseful to the victims of their crimes. Instead, they are revered by the children and a monument is built in their memory. The thinking in this book lies heavily on moral responsibilities. Is it right to use money gained through bad deeds to help others? Is stealing ever justifiable? What is wealth? Why did the robbers steal money that they did not use?

The Robot and the Bluebird

Concepts: Identity, love, survival, sacrifice.

The robot has a broken heart that cannot be fixed, so he is sent to the scrap yard as rubbish. He invites an exhausted bluebird to nest in the cavity that his heart once filled and the fluttering of the tiny bird gives the robot new purpose and energy.

The robot goes on to sacrifice itself in order to protect and shelter the bird while transporting it on the long journey south.

The book allows children to explore the nature of life itself. What is it that makes us human and how does a robot differ? It allows the children to think about the meaning of consciousness of man and machine from the starting point of what makes a robot think? Can a robot think or feel? What is love and why do we make sacrifices?

The Island

Concepts: Ignorance, tolerance, fear, human rights.

This powerful story centres on a community disturbed by the unexpected arrival of a stranger. The stranger is different and the islanders are faced with the dilemma of how to deal with the conflict of obligation and their instinctive fear of 'the different'.

This book presents obvious concepts for discussion, such as xenophobia, human rights and racism. But it is not until young people actually ask the questions that they begin to understand the complexities of human behaviour. It is very easy to say 'why didn't the islanders treat him equally', but in order to answer this question, they must first explore the issue of equality and understand and possibly challenge their own reasoned responses to the question 'How would you react if you were frightened for the safety of your loved ones?'

Case studies

A sample of case studies from these books and others follows to give a more thorough overview of how books create philosophical thinking, questioning and dialogue. These case studies serve to give a taste of what it feels like to be a thinking participant and a facilitator of enquiries.

The case studies show where children and facilitators struggle to find the words, clarify meanings and work together to move on in their thinking. It will illustrate the differences that age and experience make to the dialogue. The sophistication of the Year 5 children is a dramatic contrast to the beginnings of language development of the younger children. But it is the desire to work together and the enjoyment of this liberation of thought in the community of enquiry that shines through. Most importantly, all the dialogues show what our children are capable of when faced with challenging stimuli and will inspire you to work in this way with the children in your charge.

When a Monster is Born

Acle Primary School Key Stage 2 enquiry – This enquiry was facilitated by Maria Cornish

Facilitator (F):	Let's talk a little bit about what makes a human, human. We might touch on the difference between monsters and humans. We looked a little bit at what if a monster looked like a human and sounded like a human, and was brought up like a human, and Sam actually said 'they wouldn't be human'. . .
Children:	Yes!
F:	What I am interested in is Why not? What is it that makes a human a human?
Lydia:	A human is a living, speaking, warm blooded animal that was made by two humans – a girl and a boy
F:	Usually a girl and a boy. . .
Lydia:	Yes. Usually. Mostly
F:	Do you mean that there are partners that aren't female and male but that actually end up having children?
Children:	Yes!
F:	But you still need a female and a male to create life – but they might not end up looking after the children?
Children:	yes
F:	OK, one of things you said was about speaking – if I couldn't speak does that make me not human?
Lydia:	No because crows can speak!
F:	OK let's let Lydia qualify
Lydia:	It's really hard to think because most people in the world can speak
Other children:	I see what she's saying there

Sam:	How does that count as human though? It could be a monster that can speak breathe and be warm blooded and the rest?
F:	That's interesting Sam, so which of those makes it different from the monster?
Lydia:	Well you don't normally see a monster walking down the street
Other children:	How do you know?
F:	When was the last time you saw a zebra walking down the street?
Lydia:	Never, but you are more likely to see a human than a monster
F:	OK has any one got anything to build on Lydia's ideas? This is really tricky people this is really hard. So go on then Joe?
Joe:	I think nothing can change a human . . . if he was like a monster and made friends with a human he would feel really bad about it because he was a monster and not a human?
F:	Right you said right at the beginning 'nothing can change a human' – I didn't quite know what you meant by that
Joe:	If it was like a monster and a human they are different things. You can't change really can you?
F:	I don't know. What's your opinion? Pretend I am an alien from outer space – I want you to tell me what a human is. Anybody got anything else that can build on it?
Bronte:	A human is made of unique body parts. You've got like lungs, heart, that only humans have
F:	Well that's like saying 'a human is a human', 'a human is made up of humanness' – well I want to know what that human IS . . .
Bronte:	An animal has heart and lungs
F:	Is there a difference between an animals and a human then?
Child:	Humans can't come in yellow and black skin can they?
F:	You mean like a leopard? Well neither can a rabbit . . .
Joe:	But we want difference! I'm different to everybody in this room
F:	But tell me why you would qualify as a human rather than anything else

Isabel:	An animal can be different – it could be more hairy or have a longer tail. A person can be different, like having chubby cheeks but they could just be like a normal person going to work. A monster could speak like a human and act like one
F:	Well what does that mean 'acting like one?'
Isabel:	You are trying to impersonate a human to make yourself more natural as a human
F:	OK, if I was going to impersonate a human what would I do?
Jacob:	You would be like . . . could you put on some sort of disguise? You could put yourself in this person going to work
F:	So I would make myself look like a human. So there's the picture of a human – and I would make myself look like a human. What else would I have to do or be in order to be human or is that enough?
Toby:	You would have to get all different clothes because we all have different clothes
F:	OK let's build this up. I have to make myself look like a human; I have to have human clothes on, what else would I have to do?
Ben:	You'd have to act like a human
F:	Right, what does acting like a human mean?
Harry:	A typical person would be posh, standing up straight, wearing a suit or something like that
F:	Harley, what else makes a human?
Harley:	I guess if you saw a monster in a human suit . . . humans have manners
F:	OK. So humans need . . . this is what we've got so far, just think you can add to this . . . a human needs a human body, it needs to look like a human, it needs bones, so it needs all of the body, the skeleton, the blood and the heart. And it needs manners
Libby:	And feelings
F:	It needs feelings. So is there anything else that I need to be a human?
Beth:	They need emotions. But if they have different emotions it doesn't mean they are not human it means they are a bit different
F:	OK. Is there anything that they absolutely have to have to be human? We have already said that they might have one arm or one leg or a funny toe but they can still be human . . .
Isabel:	Their breath needs to smell human!
F:	Their breath needs to smell human? What does human breath smell like?

Isabel:	All breath smells different! If you wanted you could swallow like a whole tube of toothpaste!
Toby:	A monster eats loads of stuff and never brushes his teeth
Joe:	How do you know a monster doesn't brush his teeth? They might have a really good toothbrush
Harry:	No one actually knows what a monster looks like; I'm not saying it wouldn't look like anything but then no one's ever seen one
F:	No. What we are trying to say is 'what makes a human?' What we have so far is – they have a complete human body, a skeleton, feelings, kind of manners (whatever that is, kindness maybe), they need warm blood,
Joe:	DNA!
Benjamin:	That means they feel stuff, like humans feel stuff
F:	What do you mean, feel as in touch? Or feel as in . . .?
Libby:	Like if it rains they can feel water on their arm
Ben:	Like Libby said they can feel stuff, but they might have extra senses like 20/20 eyesight. Say they had really strong senses like really good eyesight or smell. Like say there was a cheese like a mile away? A human obviously couldn't smell that – but he could. You would have to do something or try and act normal
Sam:	How do you know?
Ben:	I am saying he might, I'm not saying he HAS, I'm saying he MIGHT
Harry:	Yes because they might have to learn how to actually be human and live in a house
Dylan:	We were talking about an alien being a monster – I wouldn't call it something in disguise
Lydia:	Well we were talking about what you actually need to be a human well most people have hair on their heads, totally different from like animals. Animals have fur or feathers
Ben:	We are animals!
Libby:	Some animals have like that disease where they have no hair on them
F:	Seriously do you think hair on your head defines humans? Do you think that's the thing?
Children:	No!
Sam:	It's DNA
Dylan:	You can't disguise your DNA! You can disguise your looks and your personality but you can't disguise your DNA

Ben: Why would someone find out your DNA unless you needed something like an injection?

F: It doesn't matter why you would want to do it, you're saying if you wanted to say 'this thing in front of me is human' you would look at the DNA – nothing else, yes?

Ben: Because you have like annual injections every three years, a monster's not really going to get away with it is he?

Joe: He doesn't have to have an injection! He could just walk off and say 'I don't have injections!'

Ben: If he doesn't feel well he's not going to know how to book appointments for doctors and stuff. He won't even know what it is

F: Don't you think there are some humans who don't know how to book appointments?

Dylan: Because some children have disabilities and some parents have disabilities and they won't know how to book an appointment or something

Lydia: If the monster had a friend he might ring the doctors up for him and say 'oh, he needs an appointment'

Sam: He wouldn't want to go would he?

Ben: He might take his monster friend

F: OK I am going to stop you now and I am going to ask you – if you would prefer to be a human come and sit on this side of the circle, if you would prefer to be a monster, as we have defined it today, that side of the circle

(Children decide and move)

Lydia: Can I sit in the middle?

F: No, you have to choose

Lydia: But I don't know!

F: You have to make a choice – even if it isn't perfect

(Children move)

F: OK what is it that makes it better to be human?

Joe: I think that if you are a monster most people will be afraid of you. In their world they think we're scary and in our world we think they are scary

Sam: I agree with Joe because if you are a monster you won't really get friends because you are really scary

Benjamin: on planet Earth you probably prefer to be a human, monsters wouldn't like to be known, they'd be like low profile, in forests. They wouldn't want to be seen

Harry: If a human went on to a planet where a monster came from, *they'd* want to keep low profile with their appearance. The monsters would think that they'd look funny

Beth: I would prefer to be a human because we find different ways throughout life and experience different things. But if you were a monster you would just experience the same thing

F: Why? Why do you think that?

Beth: Because I don't think they have much to do. Except walk in rooms all the time and try and scare people. Which is why I would prefer to be a human because you get to walk around and see all kinds of different stuff

F: Right you said it's easier and it's more interesting. Which one do you think is the most important reason?

Sam: more interesting

Harry: You would probably prefer to be a human if you were like an ape and you were stranded. You wouldn't want to be running round looking like that would you?

Sam: I would

Isabel: Why? Everywhere you go you would probably have people running after you

F: OK so people would be scared of you?

Beth: Especially if you went in the city

F: It would depend where you were wouldn't it? Whether you were on Earth or on the monster planet

Joe: Say you were on Earth and you were a monster and you wanted help. You would get it because you wouldn't have anyone around you

Sam: I would prefer to be human because when you are human you feel like you have other people to mix in with, but say you were a monster on planet Earth you couldn't really be yourself around humans because you would be different

F: What you are saying is that it is about alienation, you have got to keep a low profile or you will scare the humans. Let's hear from the monsters then

Ben: If you were a monster on Earth they might have super-intellect or mind control or read minds, or they might have much more high tech you don't know. Say a DS, humans have that, but the most high tech game for monster babies might be Uno or Monopoly or a high tech ray gun kind of thing, that might not be able to harm anyone but, you never know?

Dylan: Like Harry says you wouldn't really like to go walking round like a big jelly monster on Earth but if you humans were to go to the monster planet they might say 'oh no, why has he only got two eyes and ten fingers?'

Harley: I think you would be able to change your appearance

F: OK as a monster you might be able to change your appearance – why would that be a good thing?

Beth: Because you can learn like humans you can start growing into humans, you would be both. You are a monster and a human

Libby: I found it difficult to make this decision

F: Why was it difficult?

Libby: I was thinking about being different or being the same

C: You know how I am

Dylan: Well humans . . . nothing against humans, but I don't think it's right for them to be humans, it's kind of hard to explain

F: Tell me if I am wrong . . . Could it be something to do with wanting to be different?

Dylan: Yes it could be

F: Being a monster is more different than just being a different kind of human

Dylan: Yes

F: Why is that a good thing?

Dylan: I don't know it's just a gut feeling with me

F: Interesting to think about Dylan. Have a think about it, have a think about why it is better because I'm not sure you worked that one out yet

Ben: If you are a monster you are more likely to be free, because as a human you are stuck with all these jobs and if you're not doing jobs then there is children. As a monster you are more likely to be free and you can spend time relaxing

F: OK so you think monsters have more freedom because you can do what you want to do? You're not stuck in that human thing?

Libby: You could just relax and do whatever you wanted to do

Sam: As a monster you can come to the human planet and disguise yourself as a human and then go back to the monster planet and have a good time there. So as a monster I think it would be better, you would be able to do more things than just being human

F: OK so you agree with Ben?

Sam: Yes

Joe: I have gone to monsters because I believe it can be boring being a human and I believe it's good to have a change once in a while

F: OK. Harley, why did you decide to be a human?

Harley: Well I did think about being a monster but then I thought they might not be able to relax. I thought they might live less long

Isabel: Well the humans might be monsters to the monsters. We might be aliens to another person People are saying that monsters exist but how do we know?

F: We have to say they do for this conversation

Isabel: Well how do we know?

F: How do we know humans exist? How do we know we are not in somebody's dream?

Harry: We are right here!

Beth: Well I've been alive for a long time

F: Anybody want to swap? Change your mind?

(Some children swap)

Benjamin: Why? Why would you want to be a monster? Realistically if you came to Earth they would take you to a base, they would dissect you, do tests on you

Harley: They wouldn't do that! They would think that they could breathe fire, they could eat you . . .

F: OK Ben why have you moved? Why have you changed your mind?

Ben: If you are a human you just stay the same. You can't be whoever you want to be

F: Is it because we are human and you are thinking about monsters being different but if we were monsters sitting here do you think that you would be on opposite sides? 'I'm happy being a monster because nobody's going to take the mickey out of me?'

Ben: If humans dissect monsters, monsters might dissect humans

Dylan: They might do more! With one touch they might be able to take a human brain out!

F: Let's go back to the book! What age do you think this book is for?

Sam: It has some complicated words like 'monster' and 'hotel' so I think it should be for ages five or six?

Isabel: I think adults! Or for any age actually. At first it seems like it's probably for younger children but we have spent an hour talking about it so it is obviously for any age!

The Robot and the Bluebird

Key Stage 1 – 16 children aged 5–7 years

After sharing the story, I laid the concept cards on the carpet and asked the children to think about which cards might best explain the thinking behind their questions.

The questions recorded were:

- Why did the robot have a broken heart?
- Why did the bluebird love the robot?
- Why did the robot keep on going?
- Why was the bluebird friendly to a robot?
- Why did the robot let the bird live inside him?

I then explained that we were going to push our thinking into making secondary questions using the concept cards to think about the philosophical meaning

The children matched and justified allocation of the cards. Through this process, the children identified and justified the following concepts: love, power, protection, rescue, identity, bravery, choice, freedom and survival.

The children were then asked to work in pairs and choose one of those concepts to create further questions from.

The secondary questions were:

- Can a robot have a heart?
- Is a robot a real person if it can feel things?
- Can loving someone really break our heart?
- Would the bird have loved the robot if he hadn't helped him?
- Can you love someone if they have never done anything for you?
- Do people pretend to be friendly just to get what they want?

The following extract contains dialogues raised from these secondary questions:

Abbie: I think that sometimes people do just pretend to be your friend so they can get things. Like when my sisters say they will play and then actually just take what you were playing with and run off and then sometimes that means when I get cross I get told off by mummy for not sharing

Madison: Sometimes though you have to pretend like if you were poor and had nowhere to live you would be all nice to people and then they will let you stay in their house

Henry: Not all people won't, some might not trust you

Abbie: But how do you know if they are really friendly if they are tricking you or not?

F: Who do you mean?

Abbie: I mean how do we know if people are being nice or tricking us?

F: Do you mean how can we tell who our real friends are?

Abbie: Yes. I think sometimes people say to me 'you aren't my friend' but I am even if we get cross with each other

Lavelle: I think we know if you are really friends because the next day or even after dinner or maths or something you forget you were angry or jealous or whatever and then you go back to being friends

F: So can you start off by pretending to be friends and then become true friends?

Abbie: Yes I think there is such a thing as true friends because once you didn't have any friends

Tilly: Yes like when you was a baby you didn't have friends

Lavelle: You did I had friends when I was a baby I knew Danny when he was a baby

Henry: But you couldn't be proper friends because he couldn't talk and nor could you probably

Lavelle: But you can be friends and not talk, like when you watch a film at the cinema you don't talk

Olivia: Or even if your friend doesn't go to the same school and then you can only see them maybe once a year then they are still your friend

Abbie: Yes and I have even got a friend that lives in Australia

F: I have a little girl in nursery who has lots of imaginary friends. Do you think that is possible?

Olivia: Hmm well I think so, actually I don't know

F: Is a friend just a human?

Tilly: I think you can have a pretend friend because you can talk to them and stuff

George: But how do they talk back to you

F: Isn't that the same as having a friend in Australia who doesn't talk to you?

Lavelle: Well you have to be human. The robot wasn't human was he?

George: But he wasn't real

Abbie: In the story he was because he felt sad and he loved

F: Someone asked a question earlier that talked about that. Do you think a robot could ever be like a real person?

Henry: Well an android can

Olivia: What's an android?

Henry: It's a robot that is like a human in every way

F: In every way?

Henry: Well yes it has skin and things but actually no, underneath it has wires and electrics

F: What other ways might an android be different?

Henry: Well it doesn't have a real brain it's like a computer, so it only thinks what you tell it to think

F: Can it answer your questions then?

Lavelle: I think it can because it will have like Google in it or something

F: That's a way of finding out information isn't it
            Do you think information is the same as knowledge?

Tilly: Umm that's hard, yes information is things I know

F: Can you 'know' things without experiencing them?

Madison: Yes you can, I know things about dinosaurs from reading in books and films and I've never seen one dinosaur have I?

Lavelle: But how do you know dinosaurs were brown or what their skin was like because we only know about their bones

George: I think maybe we can guess by looking at other creatures but we wouldn't know unless we went in a time machine back to a million years ago

Lavelle: An android would only know about dinosaurs if it was a time machine android

F: Ok, let's think about the android again. If I told the android to love me, would it?

Abbie: No, because it hasn't really got a heart

Henry: But sometimes it could have an electric heart that beats and things you can have electric hearts

F: Can an electric heart feel things then?

Henry: Well actually I don't think you need a heart to love because it comes from your brain, you just need a brain that's where you feel stuff like happy and sad or cross

The session ended here due to time restraints. I asked the children for homework to think about the issue of whether a robot was capable of friendship

The Three Robbers

Key Stage 2 – The Three Robbers – facilitated by Maria Cornish

Acle Primary School – Norfolk – 15 Year 5s with 1–2 years' experience of P4C aged 9–10 years

Children were asked to listen to the story and to think up some questions in pairs and choose one question among them to ask.

F:	Have a look at the questions, all of them and let's think – What are the themes that you think are present in the book. Give me one word that sum up the book . . . the book's about this . . . the book's about that. For example Cinderella might be about love, it might be about revenge, jealousy etc.
Beth:	Sympathy
Toby:	kindness
Sam:	Love
Isabel:	Caring
Harley:	Anger
Benjamin:	Stealing
Harry:	Jealousy
F:	Why Jealousy?
Harry:	Because they never had the chance to have children . . . or anything like that. So they get the children and they use them instead of money
Libby:	Life
F:	Life's too big. It could mean anything. You're going to have to narrow it down. Good try
Lydia:	Curious
F:	Curiosity . . . why?
Lydia:	Tiffany was curious of the robbers. She wasn't really scared of them

The facilitator then asked children to look at their questions. Someone should start by giving their question and then the others listen and think if their question has the same themes or deals with the same issues.

Benjamin:	Why did they steal all the loot and then spend it on the children?
F:	Why did they steal it all, then spend it all?
Benjamin:	Yes, on somebody else . . . instead of themselves
F:	Has anyone got a question like that?

Beth: Why did they look after the children and become nice like others?

F: Does that link?

Beth: Yes because they spent all the money they'd stolen on the children?

F: OK, so why did they change. Why did they 'become nice' after they'd been robbers. So you think that's all connected. OK

Sam: Connected with Beth's. What was different about the orphan that made them change?

F: So it's about . . .?

Sam: It's about changing

F: What was it about the orphan that made them change? Was it something about the orphan . . . because that's an assumption

Sam: I think it's because she was excited to have them come up to her cart

F: What is a theme for those 3 questions?

Sam: Changing

F: Changing. Changing from doing one kind of behaviour to another kind of behaviour. Anybody else got a question about the change in their behaviour?

Joe: How come they used children instead of treasure? Because you know how they gave all the treasure and started using children. They spent all the money on the children . . . so there might be a connection . . .?

F: Is that to do with that theme or is it something different?

Joe: Different? I think

F: Let's have the question again. Let's see what you think. See what everyone thinks

Joe: How come instead of using treasure they used children?

F: 'Used children' did they use children?

(Joe looks a little disheartened)

F: No I'm not saying it's wrong Joe, it's interesting you've chosen that word

Joe: I don't think it's right . . . they didn't really do anything with the money and they spent it all on children

F: Is it about change or is it about spending money on children, or on other people or . . .

Joe: I think it's about change because they were stealing and then they spent their money on the children. Giving them a better environment

F: Any other questions?

Jacob:	Why did they treat the girl differently than the grown-ups that they robbed?

Here the facilitator asked whether it was about change in behaviour and child agreed. However, on reflection, it is evidently about the ways people treat children and adults and has more to do with Sam's orphan questions -- What was it about the orphan that made them change.

Dylan:	I've got a question you could ask anybody

(This refers to the way the facilitator has explained that philosophical questions can be asked to anyone, even if they haven't read the book . . . why do people steal etc.)

F:	About that theme?
Dylan:	Yes. Why do bad people . . . What makes bad people change?
F:	That's a question that sums up all those questions
Lydia:	Why did they dress the orphans in red? The robbers had black so why did they dress the orphans in red?
F:	Do you think it's significant? Do you think it's important in the story that they're dressed in red?
Lydia:	No it's not that important
	Any other questions?
Harley:	I wanted to say 'Are they good or bad?'
F:	I think that really links to what makes bad people change. If someone does something that is really dreadful (what I would say is dreadful) (and that happens to people) and they change and do things that are what I would say was good . . . are they good or bad?
Isabel:	A good person because they've changed
F:	Yes but they did these awful things in the first place
Isabel:	They've seen the error of their mistakes
Benjamin:	A bit of both really because they've seen the error of their mistakes but they've done something really, really bad because they stole all that money. But in the end they spent that money on people[.] So they actually did a good thing and a bad thing. They spent other people's money which they stole and gave it to orphans
Joe:	Do you think they knew that from the first, that they wanted to get the treasure, so that they could get the children and make the city
Benjamin:	No in the book it says that the girl asks them what they're going to do with the treasure and they said they'd never really thought about it. They didn't think about it

F: Would it have made any difference? If they had thought at the beginning we'll just steal all this stuff and we'll spend it on helping the orphans, would it have made a difference about how you felt about them in the beginning if you knew what was going to happen at the end?

Joe: They could have just got all the money and spent it but they used it to help people

Jacob: Like Robin Hood

Benjamin: Steal from the rich and give to the poor

Libby: What made them steal from people in the first place?

The facilitator clarified the argument so far and reiterated the question to those children who had not contributed.

F: Would it have made a difference about how you felt about them stealing if you knew that they were going to spend it on the orphans at the end?

Isabel: They're nasty . . . because you wouldn't just start stealing

F: Do you think it was the right thing to do to help those other children?

Isabel: No . . . I know it's weird but they should have used their own money to help them because if you steal from people it's really upsetting

Sam: Yeah . . . but why would they turn into robbers and steal the money if they had the money?

Benjamin: Most people steal because of jealousy or because they have no money . . . they're poor . . . they don't have any food

Dylan: Like that time in London when people didn't have any money and they went to steal. The time when they discovered Australia and they sent all the people there

F: Does it make any difference. Why people steal?

Benjamin: Whatever happens, they shouldn't steal. Maybe they should get charity. Maybe they should get a job. Even if they have no money they have no right to break into people's houses. My mum and her boyfriend's house got broken into and their TV, car was smashed, valuables got broken into. They shouldn't have any right to do that

F: Harry, what do you think about that? Do you think there's never any reason to steal?

Harry: Well no, not really . . . if you have somewhere to live

Sam: If you have the money, why steal?

Harry: If you have shelter, if you have food and you have drink, and you have a little money there shouldn't be any reason to steal

F:	Let's take everything away. Let's say they've got no money, or very little money, or no money for something they really need. Do you think then its justified?
Harry:	They could get a job like a car factory or a train driver or something that's very easy to do
Sam:	They shouldn't steal it. If they want more money they should earn it
Dylan:	Our parents earn money and they're might be some parents who don't earn money so why can't they just go and get a job?
Benjamin:	They could get benefits. If they don't have any money . . . it's not the best thing to do. But they should get benefits. They would get a good happy life and then get food, drink and then start working when you have a good amount of money
F:	Do you think there might be a reason that someone would steal rather than . . . Why would you choose to steal?
Benjamin:	It's easier than getting a job
Isabel:	Hang on, it isn't easier. You have to be a criminal. You'd rather get a job
Benjamin:	You'd get more money, you'd get more money
Child:	I'd rather get a job than steal
Dylan:	There are some people who are bad. But then there are some people who just don't like working and think its ok to steal money so they don't have to work
F:	Do you think they have a choice? Does everybody have a choice?
Benjamin:	They had enough money in the story. In a week they had enough money to buy a castle
Joe:	I don't think it's their choice. It's like peer pressure. You know like sometimes in America. You know like Brooklyn. There are gangs and there are little children and they like tell them to do stuff. Then they get older and they get older and then they just keep going on. The peer pressure is always doing it to them
F:	Joe's saying that there may be people who may not have the same choices because their background kind of puts pressure on them. Whether it's their friends, or their family. Do you think it would be different if we were having this conversation and all your parents were in prison for robbery?
Toby:	It would be different because it's your parents and if they were stealing you'd be really annoyed with them. Like when you see it on TV and people get arrested and you think 'Oh God, what an idiot to do that!'

Benjamin:	Your parents might think it's a really good idea to steal
F:	OK. So do you think Benjamin . . . no I'm going to ask the rest of you. Just imagine for a minute that your parents were not just saying it's alright to steal but I'm going to show you how to steal
Toby:	That's really bad
F:	I'm going to bring you up to be a thief (which does happen to some children – that's how they get into it because their families have been. Not everybody but some people. Do you think you would have the same choice as you have now? I'm going to hear from Libby
Libby:	No because they're telling me to do it
F:	OK, so why would you do it just because your parents are telling you to do it?
Lauren:	If my parents started to tell me to start stealing now, I wouldn't do it because it's illegal and you can get arrested for it
F:	What Lauren is saying is that you do have a choice, in that situation if your parents say you should do this in this way or bring you up in a certain way then you do have a choice
Sam:	If I was brought up in that way, I'd take their advice so that when I needed it the most. So if I turned out to be really, really poor . . . like if I lived on the streets would be the only time that I'd use it
Child:	You're saying that might make people steal?

(Harley tries to interject)

F:	Go on Harley. I'd like to hear from some children who haven't spoken yet
Harley:	Maybe robbers are really poor, maybe they didn't do really well. Maybe they are poor . . . they haven't got any money. Maybe they didn't do well at school
F:	Do you think that might be a motive to steal? You didn't do well at school so you might end up stealing?
Harley:	If you don't do well at school then you don't get a good job and then you're pretty badly poor
F:	So if you can't get a job, and there are people who can't get a job it can be difficult to get a job. Beth, what do you think?
Beth:	People steal because – like Harley said – people can't do it . . . like if they wanted to be a doctor and they couldn't . . . they would have to steal because they couldn't do anything else. The facilitator made a conscious effort to include everyone in the group at this point
F:	What do you think Bronte?

Bronte: Well, If people are living on the streets and they had nothing, they could just steal a little bit and people would never know

(The facilitator could have explored whether, if someone steals something and the victims never know, that makes a difference)

Lydia: If someone has severe autism or something they may not be able to get a job because of how they look, if it's something they've always wanted to do . . . like be on TV. They wouldn't be able to . . . because of the way they look . . . I think they may have to steal. They may not want to steal money they may want to steal items

Dylan: I want to go back a bit. I just think that if my dad said he wasn't very good at (I don't want to criticise him) but he's not very good at literacy . . . he's got a really good job and he gets paid a lot. I also disagree with Lydia. It's hard with Lydia because it's a bit of both . . . some people do not give jobs to people . . . how people look . . . but some people think about Billy (autistic child in the class) I know Billy will get a job

F: Do you think then Dylan, that there is always a choice

Dylan: Yes, there always a choice because if my parents said something I wouldn't follow it

F: How would you know if you've made that choice or if you've been persuaded over the years?

Child: You can't know

F: Can't you?

Dylan: It's a decision you can make, but it's a very hard decision

F: It's interesting to know, everyone, whether we have choices or not. How much we are making our own decisions and how much people have persuaded us over the years

Isabel: But everybody has a different opinion. Some people like may try to make you on their side. So like all over the world people would have all different decisions

Dylan: There's never a right answer for anything

F: Anything?

Dylan: No, not 1+1 makes 2

Harry: Dylan's not right because in literacy and maths tests you've got to get it right

Isabel: Hang on. When they started it, they only decided to make up the answer. There isn't really an answer for everything

Harley: Yes there is such thing as a wrong answer. If your best friend told you to jump off a cliff and you said yes . . . wrong answer!

Dylan: If your best friend asked you to jump off a cliff you wouldn't

F:	What if your baby brother was in the sea below? Would that change your answer?
Harley:	If it was in the bottom of the ocean it would be a bit impossible
F:	But if you thought it might be possible would it be the right answer?
Harley:	You could try
	F's final attempt to include everyone
F:	D[o] we have the choice to do what we want in our lives?
Toby:	Yes we have the choice to do what we want in our lives. If we're going back . . . if your friend says jump off a cliff . . . some people say yes, because they're friends but some people will say no, because they really think
F:	So you have to be able to think in order to make a choice
Jacob:	If someone says something to you, it's only an opinion of what they think. You can only do stuff that you want to do
F:	Is it possible to make a choice to do something you don't want to do?
Ben:	People have the choice to do what they want with their lives; no-one's controlling you. You can do what you want. You have free choice
F:	So anyone could choose to go up to Isabel now and hit her across the face?
Lots of children:	yes!
Jacob:	It would be the wrong decision
Other children:	It's your decision . . . only you can say . . . if you believed it was the right thing to do
F:	So you're saying that if someone went up to Isabel and hit her across the face and they believed that to be the right thing . . . because they didn't think she was very nice . . . would that be right?
Children:	Yes it's your opinion . . . its right for one person
F:	So right is only for one person
Child:	It's only opinion
F:	Is there ever 'right' full stop? Or 'wrong' full stop? Libby, is there ever an absolute right and wrong, good or bad?
Libby:	I don't know because sometimes you have to do the wrong thing to do the right thing
	I can't explain it

Benjamin: Say you're mum was going to die; you might have to kill someone else. So you're doing the wrong thing but it ends in the right thing

Dylan: If you had an argument with a shop of people and you need to defend yourself. But if they are picking on you, you need to defend yourself. You would be pushing yourself back. That's the wrong thing to do but it's the right thing to do to get away from them.

Isabel: If not you won't be happy

Session finished as it was the children's break time.

No!

Acle Primary School – 11 Year 5s – Key Stage 2 enquiry facilitated by Maria Cornish

The facilitator read the book and asked the children to write a few sentences about what they thought the book was about. They were asked to do this by themselves without talking to anyone else. The facilitator then asked them to work on a question in pairs.

These are some of the comments they wrote:

- 'Boy wrote letter. Important letter – discovers the war on the way home.'
- 'It looks like it is a war and he is writing to the president to stop it.'
- 'It's about a boy who writes a letter to the President about what rules he has at his school and if he had any rules. There is this boy standing in front of the letterbox and the other boy stands up for himself.'
- 'I think that the boy is a strange boy who wants to find out if there is stuff you are not allowed to do (rules) because they have rules in his school (rules about the war).'
- 'He sticks up for himself and his country.'
- 'It's an important message. It goes bad to good.'
- 'He's sending a letter to the President.'
- 'A little boy writes a letter to the President and on his way he sees lots of bad things happen. Then he says "No!" for not bullying and the bad things go good.'
- 'It's about this boy who really wants to post this letter and when he goes to the postbox there is a mean boy. The boy who wants to post the letter stands up for what is right! The letter is about rules.'
- 'I think it's about a boy who writes letters to the President to say his rules and give ideas.'
- 'It's about standing up for yourself but with words not violence.'

F:	Right, who's got the first question? What we're going to try and do is to keep linking these questions. So while people are giving these questions I want you to think about the themes. I want to do less of trying to prompt you and more of you thinking. I think all of those questions are about a key issue.
Benjamin:	Why did they hurt them and then help them?
F:	Anybody got a question that is connected with that?
Harry:	I've got the same one
F:	That was yours as well? The exact words, Harry?
Harry:	Yes
F:	Anybody else?
Bethany:	Why did the boy at the letter box be really mean to the boy posting the letter?
F:	Is that connected to this question?
Bethany:	Yes because he was really like mean to him and then he helped him by giving his hat back and giving him a ride on his bike
F:	What's the connection?
Bethany:	All the other people were being mean to them and then helped them
F:	Has anyone else got a question about being mean and then helping?
Ben:	When he sticks up for himself he sticks up for his country
F:	OK, put that into a question
Ben:	Why did the boy stick up for his country?
F:	OK, is that connected with this or is it a different theme?
Ben:	A different theme
F:	Because actually what is going to happen there, if you ask that as a question . . . you've got a theory, an idea . . . but if you ask that question we can all talk about that idea so that rather than putting it in a statement you can put it in a question so that everyone can talk about it
F:	(while writing down the question) You said originally for himself as well as his country
Ben:	Because as soon as he stuck up for himself all the people that were attacking his country helped them
F:	That's interesting isn't it? Right, have a think about what theme that might be. What's behind that question? What words. . . . Has anyone got anything that's connected with either of those? Why do they hurt them and then help them or why did he stick up for himself?
Lydia:	Why did, when he started off walking they were bad and when he came back they were good?"

F:	Is it connected with this one?
Lydia:	Yeah
F:	Ben, can you just think about your question and think if you can make a connection with Lydia's?
Ben:	Yeah. Because when he shouted 'No!' that made the other people from the other country from the war . . . they were from Germany and he was from England and as soon as he said 'No' stop it all, they stopped. He saying No and he's saying stop it all
F:	Ok, so there not about exactly the same thing but they're connected . . . like a cause and effect.
F:	Has anyone got one that is linked . . . (no response) OK has anyone got something different?
Dylan:	I've got something totally different. It has got something to do with the story but not as such . . . Why did the author put no words in?
F:	Do you think that is a philosophical question . . . is there something behind that . . . or do you think it's a literary question . . . about the way people write books . . . or something else.
Dylan:	I think both. It's Philosophical because it's about whether having words would be a good or a bad idea but it's also a literacy question because it's literacy
F:	That's a hard question to ask you because we haven't done much work on the difference between what's to do with the structure of the book and what's to do with the content of the book and where they overlap
F:	Thank you, anyone else?
	Isabel seemed tentative and Beth was encouraging Isabel to speak
F:	Beth is very keen for you to share your idea
Isabel:	It's not very good. I've got 'Why is he writing a letter?'
F:	Why do you think it's not very good?
Ben:	Because it's pretty obvious that his dad's in the war and he's writing a letter
Lydia:	It doesn't say that
Benjamin:	He's writing to the President
Lydia:	I don't think it's very obvious
F:	Can I just show you the two letters in the story
Benjamin:	One said 'Dear Roger' and the other one said 'Dear President'
F:	The first one says 'Dear President'

(The facilitator talked through and explained the pictures)

F: The last letter is showing us what he wrote originally. The author is not showing us what he wrote until the end

Benjamin: I kind of thought that. It doesn't really make sense. Why did he want to ask the President whether he had any rules? It must be connected in some way. You wouldn't just ask the President 'Do you have any rules?' It must be connected with his dad or something

Lauren: Why does he want to find out about that?

Isabel: Yeah, why was he writing the letter, because nobody would write a letter asking about there being rules at school, no punching, no pushing . . . no one would really do that

(Lots of people join in wondering about the letter)

F: That's obviously a really burning question for you . . . why did he write that letter? What was the point of it?

Benjamin: Maybe the President started a war. Maybe he's asking Why did you start the war . . . no pushing . . . no punching no killing . . . no shooting. Maybe the President declared a war against the boy's country and he's not happy about it he's *asking in a different way*: 'Why did you start the war, why are you shooting, why are you killing?'

F: Let's go back to Benjamin's point that if he wrote this letter the President started the war. Why would the boy write the letter?

Isabel: To tell him that there are rules inside school like no punching, no pushing so he thinks they shouldn't do it outside as well.

F: What do you think?

F: Let's just have your thought

Benjamin: I get it now. The boy's basically saying 'Why did you start the war?' We don't have mini fights, we don't hurt each other and he's saying why do you hurt each other and not be friendly

F: OK, thank you – hold that thought, we'll come back to it. I just want to know that everyone who's here has had a chance to put their ideas forward. Harry, did you have a question?

Harry: Yeah, mine's been said

Joe: Yeah mine as well

F: Are you sure you haven't anything to add

Joe: No it's fine it's up there

F: What about Harley?

Harley: My question is; Who is the boy in the Green hat . . . I mean it could have been . . . no it couldn't have been his brother . . . I mean he did just take his hat

Benjamin: maybe it's just a person who was walking down the road
F: Who do you think it was, Harley?
Harley: I don't know . . . it could have been someone . . . a poor person maybe . . . the boy in the red hat said 'No!' and that made the boy in the green hat give it back
Lauren: He was scared
Isabel: I think he was jealous. He was jealous that someone smaller than him could be more powerful

(The facilitator could have explored this line of enquiry)

Benjamin: I think it's just somebody from school. [H]e's just like a big bully at school. And if any small people come along he bullies them
Joe: I reckon when the boy says there are no fights in that school, I reckon there is
Benjamin: I'm talking about the story
Joe: Because even if a school's friendly, there's always some bully-ing in a school
Benjamin: Yeah I know there's loads, I'm talking about this story
Joe: Ok, I thought you were talking about this school
F: Ok, so what does this say about rules in school? Because all schools have rules
Isabel: But not many people follow them
F: Let's go back to Joe . . . all schools have rules yeah. You also have bullying. Do you think there is a school in this country, or in Norfolk or wherever that they say bullying is fine?
Joe: In this area?
F: Anywhere
Joe: I don't know because you can't say you can't bully, not out-side of school 'cause you don't have rules outside of school?
F: Don't you have rules outside of school?
Child: Yeah, the law
Joe: Yeah, the law but bullying isn't the law . . . it should be
Benjamin: The President doesn't say 'You 10 year old it is illegal for you to bully that 5 year old.' There's not that rule
Dylan: He should say that. He should be able to say that

(The facilitator could have picked up this point here . . . taken into account the difference between the accountability of adults and children)

Benjamin: Someone might be really poor and taking their anger out, someone might be really poor on other people. He would get arrested. I don't think that's really fair. Maybe there should be a rule that they shouldn't do it but I don't think it should be a law

Isabel:	You can relate that to school because if you had it as the law, if you think of our rules in school . . . there are bullies in school because nobody really follows the 'Golden Rules' sometimes as they think so. If you had a law some people would follow it . . . some people would get away with it. Because there is stuff that happens
Dylan:	There are certain rules in the law that people don't actually bother to follow like speeding
Isabel:	Yeah, people speed
Dylan:	I'm not framing my dad here or anything but he does go a little bit faster than he ought to
Isabel:	I think everybody may do that Dylan
Dylan:	Yeah, everybody . . . I'm not saying everybody has to but it's alright for everybody to speed in their life
Harry:	My mum has a car right and when she's doing 40, it's not like she's going at 100 miles per hour
Isabel:	You have to actually look at the speed. Because you can go so fast
F:	We are saying that there are some rules that are. . . .
Dylan:	Less. . . .
F:	Less followed than others

(The facilitator could have picked up on mood at this point that some rules are OK to break. However the facilitator kept it in mind for later)

Joe:	Can I go back to what I said before Dylan's bit?
F:	Yes
Joe:	I reckon if bullying . . . You know killing's a law? No one does killing really in schools. So I reckon if they did bullying as a law it would be the same as killing, so no one would bully
F:	So are you saying Joe that if it was a law for the whole country, not just a school rule then it wouldn't happen? You're saying that children don't kill children in school because there's a law against it and because there isn't a law against bullying that's why people bully
Joe:	Yes
Benjamin:	If there was a law against bullying maybe children would come up with another way to hurt children's feelings
F:	What do you think Harry?
Harry:	With Dylan's idea with like speeding and like breaking the law, yeah . . . it depends how the car is, because my mum's car is really small and when you're doing like 40 it's like you're doing at least 70
F:	So what's your point?

Harry:	It depends how powerful the car is
F:	OK, does it make any difference? Say if the police came up and you say 'Oh I didn't realise that I was travelling over the speed limit.' Would it make any difference?
Dylan:	It does, yes it does. I think it does make a difference. Right, say you've just taken your car in for an MOT and they say that's all fine and they don't notice that it's not working properly and it passes and you drive at what you think is the speed limit and it's faster. You get stopped by the police and he notices that your speedometer is wrong. I could say 'The MOT people let me pass'
F:	That would be a very unusual situation. Let's say 2 drivers going down the road, one of them because they think it's fine to speed. They know that they're breaking the law, they know what the speed limit is, but they're in a hurry and they're breaking the law on speeding ok? That's quite a common thing to do. People know that they are speeding but they speed anyway. And they cause an accident. Right now same situation going down the road, the person isn't meaning to speed, it's a new car, they don't realise and the same thing happens and they cause an accident. Should those 2 people be treated the same?
Children:	Yes!/No!
Isabel:	Yes, because they're both hurt
Lauren:	No. [B]ecause they didn't know
Dylan:	Yes because they could say I didn't realise that. Anybody could say it
F:	Are you changing your mind?
Dylan:	Yes, because it's like at school. You could say I didn't realise I was hurting them when you could have been hurting them
Benjamin:	I think it's ok to break the law, not in like a serious way but say your son got stabbed by someone and you needed to go to hospital and you speeded
F:	So . . . what if your son gets very badly injured and you're speeding to get to the hospital and you knock someone down
Benjamin:	Yeah, it would be my fault . . . it depends how good your lawyer is.
Joe:	You're still breaking the law. The police don't care
F:	Should they care?
Joe:	They're still going to give you a fine and take you to court
F:	Should they care. Should they see it differently or not?

Benjamin:	What if you had 4 mins to live and you couldn't get to the hospital
Joe:	They're not going to care
F:	Benjamin said something that was some laws are ok to break. Are there certain circumstances when it's ok to break the law?
Ben:	You can break some laws like if you're driving to the hospital and your son has a broken leg you wouldn't care about speeding you'd just drive
F:	You might not care about the speed limit Ben, you're absolutely right, you might be so upset that you don't care about the speed limit but is it ok then to speed?
Ben:	If your son and daughter's in danger and you love 'em to bits you'd do anything
F:	I know you'd do anything but is it right to do anything?
Isabel:	No because it isn't right, I know it sounds weird, but it isn't right because other people probably don't speed to get their children to hospital, so why would you speed? Plus you'd call an ambulance because you'd be breaking the law and they'd stop you and it would make it longer
F:	So you're saying that they could make it longer. You said something else which was interesting which was that not everybody would break the law, that not everybody would speed to get to the hospital with their injured son so why should you?
F:	Does it make a difference what other people are doing?
Beth:	I think you should do it, because if your son or your daughter is at the risk of dying, you'd want to save them rather than worry about breaking the speed limit
Harley:	I strongly disagree with that actually because if your son or daughter was in trouble and you had to jump off a cliff to save them that would probably be kind of the wrong thing to do
F:	Why Harley?
Harley:	Because it's like sacrificing yourself in a way. If you get dead and then your daughter doesn't and then your husband's still alive and they'll have no-one to look after them
Joe:	Are you saying that if you're the person in hospital you would need to kill someone else to save that person? That's like saying breaking the law to save them. That's like basically saying the same thing. Whatever law it is, it's still the same law. Breaking the law on speeding is like breaking the law on killing.

F: What are you saying? In order to do something . . . to save someone . . . you shouldn't break the law because it's just as bad as. . . . I didn't quite understand

Joe: Yeah, that's it!

(The facilitator could have got Joe to clarify his statement as she wasn't sure what he was saying . . . he was saying something around the ideas that all laws have equal validity which is an interesting concept that could have been explored)

Harley: You shouldn't break the law because you could get arrested

F: Is there any other reason not to break the law?

Harley: There is one reason why you might need to speed. Your mum might be in hospital and you have to drive to her and you might speed

F: OK, I want to move on, because otherwise we're going to go round in circles. Some people are saying it's ok to break the law in what you would class as an emergency. Some people are saying No, it's not ok. Can you decide where you stand on that point. Make your decision

(The facilitator then gave them an option of standing if they agreed that there were certain circumstances when it was OK to break the law and staying seated if they disagreed)

Benjamin: I can't decide. It depends on what law

Joe: I can't make a decision

F: Yes you can. It is not a final decision. It's a decision for this moment. What is your gut reaction to that statement?

Benjamin
and Joe: Standing

F: You've got reservations. That's fine. But Ben thinks . . .? (he's sitting down)

Ben: I'm kind of like on both sides. It's bad if you break the law for no reason. You should get fined. But if it's an emergency and you speed . . . fine

F: OK it doesn't generally matter by law why you're speeding . . . if you're all saying that there are certain circumstances when the law should be broken why do we not have that in our system?

Benjamin: They would do that, but people could lie.

F: Do you think it would be better to have one law: Don't speed! or a series of different laws that say if you're speeding for this reason this happens, for another reason, this happens . . .

Isabel: If you had different laws you'd have everybody speeding and making up excuses. People would lie. Then they use loads of police trying to figure out what was going on

F: So it would be really complicated and you'd have to work out what was going on

F: Do you think that there are any laws that you think that you should absolutely never break?

(The facilitator then asked the children to write down a rule or law that should never be broken under any circumstances)

They wrote down:

- Do not kill wildlife
- No terrorism
- Don't kill anyone
- Don't blow up the Universe
- Don't blow up the world
- A teacher should not take anything that belongs to a pupil.

The facilitator explained that they would talk about each rule and decide as a group if it should go in the rule book or go in the bin (the majority would decide).

F: Right we're going to hear your ideas. Remember that once you've shared your idea it belongs to everyone. If that idea goes in the bin, it is not you that goes in the bin, it is that idea. No need to get upset. You may want to adapt the idea as we go along. You need to justify the idea if you want it in the Rule Book. You might decide actually the idea I originally had won't go in because it doesn't stand up to scrutiny – that's fine. That's why we're here. To test our ideas with others. We can have all of them in there, or none of them in there – it's up to you.

Benjamin: Mine is not to blow up the universe

Dylan: Why though?

Benjamin: Well because if you blow up the universe everything in the universe would die

F: Is there ever a circumstance when blowing up the Universe would be OK?

Joe: Yeah. What about if you know that you're going to die so everyone's going to die? So you have a choice about blowing up everything or having aliens kill you

F: So Joe is saying that there might be a circumstance where it might be better to blow up this and all the planets in the universe rather than have death in another way. Why would that be better?

Joe: Because if aliens would kill you they would turn this universe to theirs and take over the planet

Isabel: You probably wouldn't want the aliens to kill people on their own. So why doesn't it all happen at once? Get it over and done with!

F: So Isabel is saying that better to get it over and done with to avoid another death

Dylan: Would you tell people? Would you tell people you were going to blow up the universe?

(Some discussion about this question. No definitive conclusion reached productively so it went in the bin)

Ben: My rule is Terrorism is wrong

F: What would you define terrorism as?

Joe: It's about religion. What's the point of religion? It doesn't mean anything

Lauren: Yes there is

F: Joe, I need to stop you Joe you have to be really careful in these situations when you talk about things like religion . . . people's

	culture, people's religion. It's important to be respectful. You have a right to your opinion but you have to be respectful
F:	Are you defining terrorism as people killing people because of what they believe in? You're saying it's never ever right?
Ben:	It's right for them but not for us?
Beth:	There might be some reason. Like if someone was going to kill your mum, and then you would have to kill them to stop them from killing your mum
F:	What does everyone else think? We hear a lot about terrorism. Is there ever a reason to kill?
Dylan:	I agree with Beth. If someone was going to kill my dad and if the only way to stop them was to kill them. I'd kill them
F:	We've talked about your family. But what if it was something to defend your country? Or your religion. Perhaps if we don't have a religion we can imagine what it is like to have a religion. What if certain people weren't being treated properly because of what they believed do you think then, there would be justification for violence?
Harley:	Maybe in war. Maybe the war of terrorism? They're fighting for their own reasons. Some of them are fighting for terrorism and religion and things. I don't know if they are trying to defend themselves from terrorism . . .
F:	So we have a group of people that believe something so strongly that they feel it its worth causing hurt, disruption in order for them to . . .
Benjamin:	Yeah. Hitler started a war and we defended for our rights
Joe:	In other parts of the world he's thought of as a legend, even though he's a bad legend, there are people that think he was right
Benjamin:	Hitler wanted to take over the world and he wanted Germany to be the most powerful country but in the end Britain fought for their rights (like some people might say 'I fought for my religion') and they won. Yeah. It's terrorism. They have one religion and they have the other

(The facilitator could have challenged this)

Ben:	But they have no reason to start taking over countries
Benjamin:	Hitler just wanted to be one of the most powerful people. He wanted to be the president of the world.
Harley:	Obviously other countries looked at us and they're big countries and we're just really small so they just thought they'd help England

Dylan:	Don't kill anyone
Harry:	A teacher shouldn't take anything off a child
Joe:	Have an MOT on your car
F:	Can anyone think why we shouldn't have an MOT on your car?
Dylan:	In America they don't have an MOT
Benjamin:	Someone might not have enough money. Say it's a million pounds . . .
F:	It isn't
Benjamin:	Say it is
F:	So should they drive the car if they haven't got an MOT? Is there any justification to say that you should drive a car that isn't safe?
Benjamin:	If you crashed into a car and they were covered. You wouldn't learn from it because you would have your damages paid for

(The children voted and it went in the rule book)

The Island

Acle Primary School – 15 Year 5s – July 2011, facilitated by Maria Cornish

The children were read the story and then had to make questions in pairs

F:	Let's have the first question.
Benjamin:	Why did they say he's 'not their kind'?
F:	Has anybody got a question that's like that?
Dylan:	Why didn't they like him?
F:	You think that's connected. Why do you think that's connected?
Dylan:	They may not like him because he's a different kind
Bronte:	Why did they treat him differently?
F:	And you think that's connected . . . why?
Bronte:	It's related because if they didn't like him they'd treat him differently . . . or something like that
Beth:	Why did they help him?
F:	What, the fishermen? Is that connected with this or is it about something different
Benjamin:	Yes it does connect

Beth:	Yes, because he's different and if he was their kind they probably wouldn't have helped him because he would know how to look after himself
F:	So what are these questions all about? If you had to have a theme about what these questions were about, what would you say?

(The facilitator goes over the questions)

Various children:	Strangers, people not liking people who are different, what is kindness?
F:	Someone said it's about differences. It's about people liking or not liking, helping and not helping. Whether people like you or not because you're different. This one is about the differences and people's behaviour. Has anyone got a question that goes with that theme of difference and how people behave in response to that?
Isabel:	Why did they want him to go?
F:	So you think that is to do with being different?
Isabel:	Yes
Libby:	Why did the villagers take the man in then send him back?
F:	Do you think it's to do with differences or do you think it's something else?
Libby:	It's a bit of both
F:	What else is happening in that question?
Libby:	It's different because they let him in and then they sent him back
F:	So there's a change and nobody asked about the change. Others have asked about why they did a particular thing, but you've asked about why they changed their minds. So what's that question about? I think it's less to do with difference and rather about something else
Dylan:	Is not a bit like friends? You're a friend with someone one week and then you fall out and end up pushing them away (not physically but . . .) and then you're not friends with them?
F:	How do you think that relates to that?
Lydia:	The villagers took the man in (like saying 'Look this is my new friend') and then they sent him back in about . . . not a couple of weeks more like a year

F: So why . . . Libby – try and answer your own question. Why did the villagers take him in and then send him back?

Libby: They took him in because he didn't have anywhere to go . . . I don't really know why they sent him back

Sam: They sent him back because he was no good at any of the jobs. He couldn't really do anything there

Benjamin: Yeah, but if they were friends with him, why did nobody like him? They said 'Oh he eats with his hands . . .'

Isabel: Only the fisherman liked him

(The fisherman in the story persuades the villagers to take the stranger in)

F: I think there is a difference in this question because they had a change of mind

Dylan: At the beginning everyone agreed with the fisherman and then gradually everybody changed and disagreed with him

Bronte: Maybe they just felt that there wasn't a place for him, they didn't know who he was they thought that he could have done anything. He could have done something bad, he could have killed someone. He could wreck the restaurant, wreck the grocery etc.

Joe: I think they are worried about keeping him, not so much because he might murder them, but more because he'd always be in their lives forever. He's be stuck in the corner, and they'd always be seeing him, and they don't want to be seeing that every day

(The facilitator could have asked pupils 'Why?' in response to Joe's statement)

F: What is the main reason for the villagers sending him away? Is there an emotion that is motivating them?

Sam: Scared. They're scared because when they're talking about it in the story, they're starting to get a bit scared of him. Their fears would start to get into nightmares

F: Does everyone agree, or was it something else?

Benjamin: Yes it's fear . . . For the children, because in the story the mother said 'If you don't eat your soup, he'll come and eat you'

F: Was there any evidence for that fear? Had he done anything that made them have that fear?

Toby: When he came into the town . . . that, like, scared the children and the parents

F: Why?

Toby:	There was no warning that he's come in. He just came in without any warning
Isabel:	He acted strangely
F:	So if you walked into a village by yourself and you hadn't 'warned' anybody, would people be scared of you?
Toby:	It would depend on what you looked like
F:	So it was what he looked like?
Benjamin:	Yes, but if there was someone who looked a little different, you wouldn't run. 'Ah get out of here!'
Isabel:	It said that he was French or something in the book
Sam:	Foreign
F:	So he was foreign. Why would that make them frightened?
Isabel:	Because he came from a different country
Joe:	I reckon they don't know where he's been. I reckon they are frightened because they don't know him
Dylan:	If there's like a new Teaching Assistant and they're in our class . . . I don't know what it is. I'm not scared of like asking them questions. . . . It's not fear . . . I don't know what it is
F:	Can anybody help Dylan with that?
Dylan:	It's nerves because you don't know what they're going to be like. She may be like really hard or she could be really nice
Isabel:	You don't know, you've got no clue where they live or anything. If a foreign person walked in, you'd be worried. Is she nice or not?

(The facilitator clarified the themes of difference and fear etc. and then asked for any other question. She wanted to get everyone's questions in before she explored their ideas further)

Toby:	Where did he come from?
F:	OK, Toby I'm going to query this question. We know each other well and you know I think you're brilliant and I want other people to see that when they read the book they can see the difference between the types of questions that come up. So I want to talk about why you think I might have doubts about that question as far as philosophy is concerned?
Beth:	Because you can't really talk about it. All you can say about it is different places like . . . he came from France, he came from Germany
Benjamin:	It doesn't have an answer
Lydia:	It's like a mystery you'll never solve. It would be better to ask about the character of the people
Dylan:	But that man is a character
Sam:	You're kind of guessing an answer but you're not talking around the ideas of why things happen.

(The facilitator made a judgment about the nature of that question. She was confident that the child was asking simply 'What country' but could have pursued it further. She was also confident that she had worked with the child for 2 years and checked, and had confirmed, that he was not upset by his question being targeted)

F:	Any other questions?
Isabel:	Why did the villagers put him in the goat house thing?
F:	Can you try and answer that?
Isabel:	Because they didn't like him because he wasn't like other people
F:	Is it linked with the previous themes or not?
Isabel:	Yes it's linked with people treating him in a certain way because he was different
Libby:	Why didn't they like him just because he was foreign?
F:	That's interesting Libby, because in that question you've put an assumption. You've assumed that they didn't like him because he was foreign
F:	OK anyone I haven't heard from?
Harry:	Why did they put a huge wall around the island?
F:	Is this linked?
Harry:	I'm not sure?
F:	Can anyone else help?
Beth:	I think it's separate because they didn't build the wall around because he was different. It's because they don't want people discovering their island
F:	OK . . . has it got anything to do with that man?
Lots of children:	No, not really!
Dylan:	But maybe it has though, because they thought no-one had found their island, and then he came and so they thought maybe people can find our island. So they ought to build a wall round it. But then, why would they build a wall round it because that would make it even more visible?
Benjamin:	Yes, because if somebody was sailing by, they'd see a giant, enormous wall and say 'I'm going to see that!'
F:	But let's think about their motives for building it
Lydia:	He might come back! He might go away and tell someone about it and say: 'Can you go and fight or something[?]'
Joe:	It's to protect it from other people like him

Toby:	Because if there was something like a war or some-thing, that might protect them or something
Ben:	Why did the stranger build a raft in the first place?
Joe:	It's the same story in a different island
Isabel:	I think he was going on his holidays
Benjamin:	He might have been travelling in a stormy sea
Sam:	It looks like he was trying to play around in the sea. It went off and he couldn't stop it

(The facilitator clarified that the man was 'washed ashore' by 'fate and ocean currents' so he hadn't landed there on purpose)

Benjamin:	You wouldn't choose to go out to sea on a raft. I think he could have been playing by the beach and it could get swept away
Sam:	He might just be travelling to different islands
Benjamin:	He might be poor
Bronte:	He might just think 'I don't care, I want to die.' He could live in a jungle and couldn't get a proper boat, so he built a raft
F:	Any last questions?
Harley:	Why did he send him away and then burn the fisher-man's boat?
Joe:	Because it was the fisherman's fault. He was the one that put them in that situation
Lydia:	But he was only trying to be nice
Dylan:	But Joe, if they thought it was the fisherman's fault and they didn't like the man why didn't they burn the man's boat and possibly him too
Joe:	I know, but didn't they do something to the man?
Sam:	But if they burned the man's boat, he wouldn't have been able to get back out would he?
F:	What does a fisherman use his boat for?
Lots of children:	To fish!
F:	Ok, why does he fish?
Benjamin:	To get food
Toby:	To feed the island
Bronte:	To get his money, to live
Dylan:	They didn't want fish out of the sea that the man had come in anymore
Harry:	But they need to survive. Are you going, if you're sacking someone, burning their ship, who's giving you food?

F:	So what is their motivation for burning, the fisherman's boat? Let's think about the themes behind this
Isabel:	Anger
Toby:	Protection
F:	How is that protection? What was the fisherman going to do? This didn't go anywhere
Benjamin:	Fear, because he could have brought the man back in
Joe:	I think it's 'wealth', because when they do the boat, he can't like make another one, and he can't make money
F:	Why would they do that?
Joe:	They take everything away from him. He won't have money because of what he's done!
F:	So what's that called when you do those things?
Dylan:	Disagreement

(The facilitator talked about punishment. The facilitator recapped the questions and attempts to find the key issues that are behind the questions by asking the children to take their questions away from the book. This is possible as there has been a lot of talk about the thinking behind the questions so far)

F:	What are the first lot of questions about? These questions are all about the book. If you had to ask a question of someone who hadn't read the book what would it be?
Joe:	Why do people treat people differently?
Benjamin:	Why do people judge people because of their looks?
Lydia:	Why do people stereotype people?
F:	What's the next set of questions about?
Lydia:	Why do people go to different countries?
F:	OK, what about the building the wall question?
Isabel:	Why do people build walls?
Ben:	Why do people need privacy?
Joe:	Or protection
Toby:	You're more likely to see the island with the wall!
F:	Yes, that's a flaw in their plan I guess. Look around in this school we have a fence all the way round.
Bronte:	To keep people out
Ben:	To keep us in
Isabel:	Yes it says 'This is my space'
Beth:	Why do people reject people?
Libby:	Why do people take it out on another person?
Lydia:	Why, if you fall out with someone, do you get angry and break something of theirs?

Benjamin: It's not just his fault, it's everyone's fault, and if they didn't want him there they would have shoved him out in the first place

(The facilitator then asked the children to vote for one of the main issues to talk about by asking them to only raise their hand if they really had something to say, otherwise keep their hand down.

They voted for the issue about why the fisherman was punished for helping the man.)

Harley: I think it was nice to be generous to the man but what he gets back is something bad

F: So what do you think about that?

Harley: I think, like, you do something good and you get something bad back . . . it doesn't normally happen. If he had said 'No we don't want you here! Go away!' Everyone would have carried on with their lives. As he didn't, it just changed for them

Sam: He helped someone, but he helped the wrong person. . . . Well, to the other people, he was the wrong person

F: Do you think it's possible to help the wrong person?

Sam: To those people, because they didn't like him. He was the wrong person

F: Let's think about ourselves. What do you think about that?

Benjamin: It's like saying if a random person from another country comes into your house and says 'Can I stay here?' and you say 'Yeah, sure, why not?' then they broke all the stuff, they were rude, they ate with their hands, then the person who had asked them to stay, would obviously get punished.

F: OK, was that the case in this case? That he was rude etc.?

Isabel: He wasn't rude

Benjamin: He was different to everyone else. Nobody was the same as him. So they might have thought that's a rude person

Lydia: But everyone's different. Not everyone's the same. Like in here, everyone's different

Dylan: I'm totally different to most people

Lydia: Yeah. Dylan likes the Beatles and stuff. Bronte likes artwork

Dylan: But I don't get treated badly. People don't come into my house and burn my things

Lydia: It's like if someone comes to our school. (She names a new child at the school). He didn't start off by getting treated badly. It's not like he's been rejected from his old school . . . so 'Let's reject him as well!'

Isabel:	Yes, you can't treat people badly, because some people might like him
F:	OK. Do you think the villagers were right to do the things they did to the stranger?
Benjamin:	Some things that they did were good, like they fed him. He's poor, he had to work, but then he was beaten up when he went to town and everyone was panicking. Nobody said 'He can stay with me!' They just shoved him in a corner with nothing
Libby:	At the beginning of the book he seemed like he was confused. He didn't know what he was doing
F:	Do you think the fisherman behaved in a correct way?
Toby:	Yes, because you wouldn't just walk up to a person (because he was foreign), you wouldn't just walk up to a person and say 'Oh go away, you're not allowed in here!'
F:	But do you think people do that?
Lydia:	Yes, like if you go to Greece and they don't like you because there's a war going on. They don't like you to go to like the Arabian countries
Benjamin:	It's like a park really. Like they'd say 'No dogs allowed!' and if there was a country and it said 'No French allowed', 'No German people allowed'
Joe:	That's racism
Isabel:	Sometimes people are jealous of other people. That's why they're horrible

(The facilitator told the children said that although there were restrictions on people coming into a country that we also have laws that say you can treat people differently because of where they come from.)

Joe:	Yes that's illegal. Racism is illegal
Joe:	You know what Toby said about how you wouldn't say 'No, you can't come into our country', well what do you think racism is? Because people do do it
F:	OK, explain Joe, what racism is
Joe:	OK let's say someone came from . . .
Isabel:	Britain
Joe:	Africa. Let's say someone came from Africa to this school. Then some people are going to say something. That's what racism is . . . it's like bullying and stuff
F:	Bullying because of what?
Joe:	Because of what they look like, where they come from and their religion

Benjamin: If you go to a school with everyone with different coloured skin they might treat you differently to everyone else. That's racism. So if everyone gets given an ice-cream, you might be given, . . . I don't know . . . a pea!

(The facilitator sums up by saying that we know that racism exists and that Joe had said that racism was a theme in the book. She then went on to ask why people behave in a racist way)

F: Some people behave like that, some people don't. Some people couldn't care less what country you come from

(The facilitator explained of a personal experience of visiting another country when strangers had helped someone from a different country they didn't know)

Joe: I reckon some countries are like that, but just say somewhere, like Afghanistan, you went into the place, you walk down a street, you wouldn't get that

Toby: We're at war with them

Sam: They'd be scared!

Toby: They'd go on to the other side of the street to keep away from you

Isabel: They might think you are a spy

F: OK, racism happens everywhere. It doesn't just happen in England it happens everywhere. What I want to know is what is it that causes people, not to just be a bit nervous because we often feel a little nervous if we don't know someone, but to behave in an aggressive way

Libby: It might be jealous because of what they've got, or that they're pretty

Joe: I honestly think it's depends on the country they live in

F: What do you mean?

Joe: Like if it's a war or something. Like us in World War 2. If we went to Germany, they just wouldn't treat us well

F: Why?

Toby: Hatred. Go back what to Joe said about wars. You'd hate them

F: Any other reasons?

Sam: I don't understand why people should

Lydia: They might think that certain people are changing their lifestyle. I don't think it's true, but they might think that

Isabel:	They might say things without thinking, but they don't know that it can upset people from a different country
Toby:	Like if you say something about someone from another country that can create racism. Like if you are from England and you say something nasty about Afghanistan, that can create racism

(The facilitator asks for anyone to add anything about this subject that they feel hasn't been said.)

Beth:	They might be horrible to someone because they don't understand their religion, or where they come from
Bronte:	Because they like different hobbies. Like if someone liked swimming and someone like football they'd probably pick on each other

(The facilitator summed up the reasons for racism that they had outlined. Then asked them to evaluate the book)

F:	What did you think of the book?
Toby:	I thought it was going to be really serious and a bit like real life, but you could get quite a lot out of it and it had cool pictures
Sam:	It was serious but put into a 'not so serious' text
Benjamin:	It was really good, but I think it was a bit too serious. It wasn't like 'Yeah this is a really fun book!' But it was interesting
Joe:	It's good for Teachers, because you can get loads of information out of it, and loads of Philosophy out of it, because it's got really good themes
Harley:	I expected it to be a war book with lots of pages in it. I didn't expect it to have pictures in it. I liked the pictures
	The facilitator reminds them that they don't have to have liked it.
Libby:	I liked the book because when you read it, your brain was like, filling up with all these questions that you wanted to ask
Bronte:	I thought it was a scary book in a way. Probably because it's serious and it could happen
Isabel:	I like it because you can get a lot out of it, and you can ask a load of questions and it's good because your ideas just keep building up
Lydia:	I thought it was going to be a big book for adults but it's completely different. I think it's a good book for adults
F:	You didn't like it so much yourself?
Lydia:	I did but . . .

Dylan:	I agree with Libby but the story didn't really live up to my expectations, but I agree that all the questions built up in your mind
F:	What do you think the book is about?
Toby:	Cruelty
Ben:	How people can treat people differently just by their looks and their ways of life
Benjamin:	It's saying you shouldn't be mean, you shouldn't be racist
F:	Is it saying you shouldn't be?
Benjamin:	It's just saying it's advisable not to be, because they might be pushed out of the way and be sad
Libby:	It's like trying to show what people can be like towards others
Dylan:	Does the story have a moral?
F:	You answer that
Dylan:	Is it not to be racist?
Benjamin:	It's not saying 'You shouldn't be racist.' It's just saying 'That's how that person feels. Just imagine yourself being pushed away and being sad and crying'
Beth:	I think it didn't make sense and it was kind of random. You wouldn't just start with a man washing up at sea. You'd start with like the village first

(The facilitator reminded them about the work they did in literacy about the start of adventure stories)

F:	Do you remember when we looked at beginnings of stories that made the reader think 'What that about?'
Libby:	Yes, if it starts off randomly then you want to find out what's happened
Toby:	You want to know what's going to happen in the book

Facilitator's comments

Acle is a lovely school with talented teachers. When I came to Acle, the children I worked with were tentative with their questioning. They were very quiet and they were worried about the 'right answers'.

When I left, the head teacher commented on the children's ability to think and to ask questions and reason through ideas. Going back after a year, I was really heartened by the fact that they were so enthusiastic about doing the sessions, and that although they hadn't done any Philosophy over the past year, that they had retained the understanding of what Philosophy was all about. I am convinced it never leaves you. I am also convinced that the confidence it gives children to speak their ideas and share their questions will be invaluable in their life ahead. Certain children who shine in these dialogues were not obviously academic and yet they are given the tools to express their amazing ideas.

As a facilitator, I am critical of my interactions that are too numerous and sometimes miss the point, but I am so impressed by the children's ability to reason and justify their ideas, to abstract from the concrete and to draw parallels to their own experience. They asked questions of each other and themselves. They puzzled and said when they could not answer. They helped each other to think through an idea. They drew from their understanding of the conflicts and issues they see in the media.

My partner who read the transcripts said 'If only people could see how much children know, how brilliant they are, how much they think!' Doing P4C is not without its opportunities for teachers to make mistakes, but it is absolutely crucial in giving children a REAL voice. In P4C, children are the stars, and teachers run to keep up . . . that is how it should be . . . how it really is!

Reflective questions about using picture books for enquiry

- How can you make a collection of resources in your setting?
- How can you utilize the knowledge and experience of experts in children's literature?
- How can you ensure that picture books permeate the classroom and school environment?
- How will you go about choosing resources for philosophical use?
- In which different ways can you use picture books to add variety to sessions?
- Why are books so important for us as a society?

Resources – The book collections

This book list is designed to help practitioners gather a box of books together for using in picture book enquiries. You may wish to start off with a collection from the section 'Early Years and introductory books'. These are the classics that can also be used to stimulate thinking activities. The second section of books can be used when children show understanding of basic concepts and skills required to engage philosophically.

The final section is a collection of books for older children. These books deal with more challenging subject matters such as war, death and capitalism.

When ordering books please do try and support your local Independent booksellers. Many will make up boxes of books on approval for schools and these sellers really know their books.

Recommended picture book resources for philosophy in the primary years

Early Years and introductory books

As mentioned earlier in the chapter, these books are useful bridge fillers from early enquiries into more challenging texts. These texts can be approached in a more playful manner. Adding in active voting, movement and methods outlined in Chapter 5, early enquiries will build both the facilitator's and the children's confidence and enjoyment in using books for deeper, more progressive enquiries.

Aldo – John Burningham (Red Fox, 1993), London.
Bedtime for Monsters – Ed Vere (Puffin, 2011), London.
I am the King – Leo Timmers (Gecko Press, 2006), Wellington.
I Want My Hat Back – Jon Klassen (Walker, 2011), London.
Mother Knows Best – Jill Murphy (Puffin, 2011), London.
Not Now Bernard – David McKee (Anderson Press, 2005), London.
The Night Shimmy – Anthony Browne (Picture Corgi, 2003), London.
What Now Cushie Butterfield? – Colin McNaughton (Harper, 2005), London.
When a Monster is Born –Sean Taylor and Nick Sharratt (Orchard, 2007), London.
Where the Wild Things Are – Maurice Sendak (Red Fox, 2000), London.
Would You Rather? – John Burningham (Red Fox, 1994), London.
You Choose – Pippa Goodhart and Nick Sharratt (Corgi, 2004), London.

Books to further develop emerging philosophical skills

Boys are Best – Manuela Olten (Boxer Books, 2007), London.
Burglar Bill – Janet and Allan Ahlberg (Puffin, 2009), London.
Castles – Colin Thompson (Red Fox, 2006), London.
Edwina the Dinosaur Who Didn't Know She was Extinct – Mo Willams (Walker, 2008), London.
Good little Wolf – Nadia Shireen (Jonathan Cape, 2011), London.
Little Red Hood – Marjolaine Leray (Phoenix Yard, 2010), London.
Magpie's Treasure – Kate Slater (Anderson Press, 2010), London.
Shark & Lobster's Amazing Undersea Adventure – Viviane Schwarz and Joel Stewart (Walker, 2006), London.
Supposing – Alastair Reid and Bob Gill (New York Review Books, 2010), New York.
The Dot – Peter H Reynolds (Walker, 2003), London.
The Gift of Nothing – Patrick McDonnell (Little, Brown, 2005), New York.
The Last Noo-Noo – Jill Murphy (Walker, 2003), London.
The Paperbag Prince – Colin Thompson (Red Fox, 1994), London.
The Robot and the Bluebird – David Lucas (Red Fox, 2007), London.
The Saddest King – Chris Wormell (Random House, 2007), London.
The Story of Frog Belly Rat Bone – Timothy Basil Erihig (Random House, 2003), London.
The Three Robbers – Tomi Ungerer (Phaidon, 2008), London.
Three at Sea – Mini Grey (Red Fox, 2011), London.
Tusk Tusk – David McKee (Red Fox, 2001), London.
When We Lived in Uncle's Hat – Peter Stamm and Jutta Bauer (Winged Chariot, 2005), Basel.
Wolves – Emily Gravett (Macmillan, 2006), London.
Zoo – Anthony Browne (Red Fox, 1994), London.

The following books deal with more challenging issues and are suitable for older or more experienced children.

Angry Arthur – Hiawyn Oram (Red Fox, 1993), London.
A Sailing Boat in the Sky – Quentin Blake (Random House, 2003), London.
Death in a Nut – Eric Maddern, Paul Hess (Francis Lincoln, 2005), London.
Denver – David McKee (Anderson, 2010), London.

Duck, Death and the Tulip – Wolf Erlbruch (Gecko Press, 2008), Wellington.

Falling Angels – Colin Thompson (Red Fox, 2002), London.

FArTHER – Grahame Baker-Smith (Templar, 2010), London.

Herb the Vegetarian Dragon – Jules Bass and Debbie Harter (Barefoot, 2000), London.

How to Live Forever – Colin Thompson (Red Fox, 1998), London.

Into the Forest – Anthony Browne (Walker, 2004) London.

John Brown, Rose and the Midnight Cat – Jenny Wagner (Puffin, 2009), London.

Leon and the Place Between – Angela McAllister and Grahame Baker-Smith (Templar, 2008), London.

Magpie Magic – April Wilson (Templar, 2000), Dorking.

Moonbird – Joyce Dunbar and Jane Ray (Corgi, 2007), London.

No! – David McPhail (Francis Lincoln, 2011), London.

Paradise Garden – Colin Thompson (Red Fox, 2001), London.

Sweets – Sylvia Van Omen (Winged Chariot, 2005), London.

Tadpole's Promise – Jeanne Willis and Tony Ross (Anderson, 2003), London.

The Boat – Helen Ward and Ian Andrew (Templar, 2005), London.

The Flower – John Light and Lisa Evans (Child's Play, 2006), London.

The Heart and the Bottle – Oliver Jeffers (Harper Collins, 2010), London.

The Island – Armin Greder (Allen & Unwin, 2007), New South Wales.

The King of Quizzical Island – Gordon Snell and David McKee (Walker, 2009), London.

The Last Alchemist – Colin Thompson (Red Fox, 2001), London.

The Lost Thing – Shaun Tann (Hodder, 2010), London.

The Princess Who Had No Kingdom – Ursula Jones and Sarah Gibbs (Orchard, 2010), London.

The Short and Incredibly Happy Life of Riley – Colin Thompson and Amy Lissiat (Lothian, 2006), Sydney.

The Very Persistent Gappers of Frip – George Saunders and Lane Smith (Bloomsbury, 2001), London.

9

Putting It All Together – Thinking for Life

Home thinking – Working with parents

In order for P4C to have a long-lasting effect on children's lives, the thinking must extend beyond the classroom. This is why we should value our children's parental involvement so highly. You can, of course, use philosophy in the classroom without involving parents at home. It is a very personal decision that teachers must make. You might already have a high degree of involvement with your parents through other school activities or you may feel it would not work for your school at all.

To start off, you might want to consider how to communicate to parents how you are intending to use P4C and the benefits and value of it as a learning tool. Intake meetings for new parents are a good opportunity to communicate the part philosophy will play in their child's education. Set up a small display where you can show examples of children's work, resources and information. Home visits or visits to the classroom for new children are also ideal opportunities to share information and examples of the philosophical work that you do in the same way that you share your methods of teaching reading, writing and numeracy.

When we share philosophical thinking with parents, we aim to open up more than just communication. We are hoping to return to the values of 'family' where talk is valued and conversation is more than just the passing of comment. It is a plea for shared understanding and appreciation of each other as social beings. In order to think and talk together, adults will be modelling communication skills of a higher order. Language will draw on the past, present and future. Experiences and wishes for the future will be called upon. Talking together will be given the status it deserves in a world where silent communication seems to be taking over.

Schools are always seeking ways of both improving communication with parents and improving language skills. Sharing the work we do in philosophy can be a way of killing two birds with one stone. The following ideas are designed to help get parents on board with thinking and talking. Parents do not need specialist knowledge to understand what we are trying to achieve. They do not have to call upon things they were taught at school nor do they have to feel under pressure to deliver 'correct' answers. As a school community, you may wish to decide how you would like to start the valuable journey in shared home-school philosophy.

Suggestions for sharing philosophy with parents

Parent's philosophy notice board

This could be a large notice board or whiteboard that can be hung or placed outside at the start at the beginning or end of the day. The board could be used to display the homework question and any related points to consider. You may also find it useful to share some of the following ideas:

- A copy of the stimulus used in the most recent session along with a list of the questions the children asked and points discussed.
- A class evaluation thinking journal. This could be a notebook collating children's thoughts about the session.
- A philosophy 'character' or toy and a little board for any questions or statements from or to him. Display a note from the toy asking for the children's questions. Encourage parents to ask the toy any curious

questions too. Add comments, replies and questions from the 'character' to keep a dialogue going.

- A collection of incidental thoughts or questions that the children have
brought up at home could be noted for later discussion in the classroom. This could be headed, 'Things your children want to discuss further in classroom enquiries.'
- Examples of children's work, such as photos and illustrations from your
philosophy journals used in the sessions.
- A homework sheet. This is a write-up of what parents, carers or other
key people thought about the homework question (it is usually best to
keep this anonymous so that people feel they can be honest).
- A recording of the latest dialogue on an iPod, mp3 player or computer
and a set of headphones, although this will need to be kept inside the
school building.

The nice thing about this display area is that the content can be changed
frequently and it therefore remains fresh and exciting. Philosophy is a
constantly evolving subject and new ideas, questions and suggestions
will ensure the buzz remains. Note that all displays should also be easily
accessible to parents and visitors as well as to the children.

In addition, it is also very easy to incorporate a philosophical theme
into larger display areas, for example, work done on fairy tales or books
with a philosophical slant. Questions and thoughts that have arisen during philosophy sessions that are related to thematic displays can be pinned
around the border, hung in front or incorporated into the display itself.

You could also display the sheet of children's questions and any dialogue you may have written on the wall.

At the end of school on the day after the philosophy session, it is also
useful to put out a copy of the stimulus for parents to look at.

Parent's question board

This could be a notice board in the cloakroom or a board that you take
outside. Write an explanation for its use and assure parents that they do
not have to put their names on it. The idea is that they are free to write
any questions that they have wondered about or questions that have
arisen from the children at home. These questions could then be used in
the classroom as the basis for discussion or parents could be encouraged
to respond to each other's ideas. It is also worth you modelling the use of

this board by writing your own questions or 'Thoughts of the week' and writing or encouraging others to write their responses.

Class philosophy diary

Both these methods lend themselves well to compile a class book or diary. You will need a blank book (scrapbook size would be ideal, either bought or handmade). These books could comprise a weekly write-up of the work covered in philosophy. The content of the books could include:

- Details of the stimulus used
- A list of the questions asked by the children
- Key points of the dialogue
- The homework question
- Children's responses to homework
- Adult responses to homework
- Illustrations from thinking diaries.

When written up and put together, this collection becomes a memorable and permanent record of the children's philosophy sessions. It can be viewed by parents, carers, visitors and the children themselves. It will serve as a validation of their important thinking as they look through and comment on their work.

Invite parents to come and see a session

You may feel it is useful to invite a small number of parents (a rota or three or four parents at a time) to join a philosophy session in the later stages of the year when you and the children are comfortable with the structure of the session. The children will be able to explain the rules for the session and the format and will enjoy listening to parents' opinions and sharing their ideas. Alternatively, you may wish to ask someone to video record a session and invite parents in to watch it with the children.

Validate thinking skills

Mention the child's contribution to philosophy in school reports under literacy or Personal, Social and Health Education. Take time to discuss their thinking skills at parent's evenings and draw attention to work done by their child. It is fitting that parents see philosophy as being important to the child both socially and academically and will encourage them to value it more highly at home as well.

Parent enquiries (for the experienced facilitator)

If you have a high level of interest and support from parents in the school and you feel very confident about facilitating enquiry, you may feel that you would like to offer opportunities for interested parents to experience a dialogue with other parents. As facilitator, you could offer a session using a good-quality picture book.

Hold a book event

You may wish to invite parents and children in after school to come and look at good-quality picture books that you use for philosophical enquiry. You may also be able to invite a bookshop to bring copies of these books for parents to buy.

Sharing philosophy homework

You may wish to send out philosophy homework on a regular basis, a few times a term perhaps, or you may prefer to inform parents about what the children are doing without asking for the homework commitment.

Using home/school journals

Starting in the nursery

The purpose of the journals in the early development of home/school philosophy is to introduce the idea of communication in the home. Often parents may feel out of their depth when a child asks a challenging question such as 'am I real?' Or 'where was I before I was born?' As practitioners, we know that we do not have the answers to all the questions our children may ask. Sharing these sorts of questions together at home frees up anxiety about not explaining enough or even knowing the 'correct' answer. Whichever way we decide to present this sort of home–school thinking, it is important that we explain that there may be no definite answer. We are exploring what others think. We are rehearsing our thoughts, ideas and opinions in the safety of home and in the company of those we trust. We also explain that these books will not be 'marked' judged or critiqued.

Spelling and handwriting is not an issue, neither is it a problem if they feel they cannot write anything down. What is important is the process of dialogue, discovery and thinking together. Children are empowered to be thinking about things that grown-ups too might wonder about. To know that adults also struggle to think about difficult questions may release anxiety and encourage collaborate thinking in the home.

The word philosophy itself might at first scare some adults into thinking that this will be unduly academic or problematic. Introducing them to the ways in which we encourage their children to think means they can share the fun. When asked, many parents comment that they did not realize their child would be able to think about the issues in such imaginative and interesting ways. Sometimes, the challenge is to encourage parents to be as open and thoughtful as their children.

In our nursery, we share a class book. The book is filled with pages of questions or statements that the families are asked to look through, share and talk about together. There is a section on each page for the adults to write down what the child's thoughts are and a section for the adults to add their own thoughts too.

The book is sent home in a bag with a soft toy. In the following examples, a small owl and a fairy are used. The bag also contains a pencil case and a set of stickers for adults and children alike.

The book has an instruction sheet included in the front.

Examples
Tinkerbell's book of magic wishes

> Dear children and grown-ups,
>
> Please choose one of the spells that you would like to think and talk about together. Grown-ups should record the child's ideas and their own ideas about the wishes too. It is really helpful for the children to hear other people's opinions too and see whether they agree or disagree.
>
> Remember that there is no right or wrong answer. I am interested to hear what everybody thinks whether I agree with them or not. Children may wish to draw a picture about their ideas in the blank space provided. Please return the book bag and contents the next day so that I can find out what other people think too.
>
> have fun,
>
> Love from
> tinkerbell

(sample blank format . . . this version is usually landscape to allow enough space for the child's drawing)

Fairies should be friends with witches. Is this a good idea? Why or why not?	
Draw your ideas here . . .	
Child's thoughts about Tinkerbell's idea	Grown-ups' thoughts about Tinkerbell's idea
Name	

The following is a list of wishes. Each statement can be stuck on to a double-page spread of the journal. All the statements in the list below are available online for you to print of if you so wish.

Fairies should turn baddies into frogs
Fairies should sleep all day
People should use magic wands like fairies
People should be as small as fairies
People should fly like fairies
Babies should never grow up
People should all look exactly the same
People should live in the woods
Fairies should go to school
Fairies should live in houses like people
Fairies should only ever eat sweets
Fairies should be friends with witches
Fairies should be as big as people
Children should keep fairies in their pockets
Children should go to fairy parties every night
Babies should wear flower petal clothes

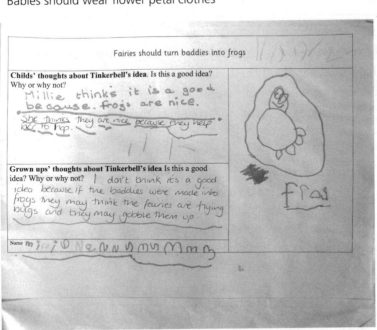

A different version of the Tinkerbell book is the Baby Owl book. We had been using Baby Owl as a stimulus and aid to help children understand

what clever thinking was. It seemed a natural progression to use him as
our home-school-thinking toy.

Baby Owl's book of wise rules

People should live in nests Is this a good idea? Why or why not?	
Child's thoughts about Baby Owl's idea	Draw your ideas here
Grown-up's thoughts about Baby Owl's idea	
Name	

Can you give reasons why Baby Owl thinks these might be wise rules?
What would happen if these rules were true? Can you say whether you
think they are wise or not wise and why?

The following is a list of statements that can be included in the
book:

Birds should not fly
People should fly like birds
All birds should talk
Birds should live in houses like people
Birds should go to school
People should live in nests
Babies should hatch out of eggs
People should look after all animals
People should have feathers
Birds should wear clothes
People should catch or find all their food

Birds should be bigger than people
People should only sing all their words
All birds should have pink stripes
People should all look exactly the same
There should be no cats
People should have long beaks
Birds should chase cats
Birds should only ever eat sweets
People should be the size of birds

Key Stage 2, ages 7–11 years, class philosophy journal for home-school thinking

You may wish to start a class philosophy journal along similar lines to the ones we do in the foundation stage and Key Stage 1. The following are samples of questions that you could start with.

How do we know . . .?

- That we are not toys?
- We are who we say we are?
- People are cleverer than animals?
- Oranges are orange?
- That we are not all asleep having the same dream?
- That the news is not a soap opera?
- That aliens do not live among us?
- That animals do not have dreams and wishes?
- That there is not someone else living an identical life to us?
- That we control our own actions?
- That our thoughts are original and unique?
- That the past really happened?
- That the world will still exist tomorrow?
- That we have not lived before?
- That time travel has not already been invented?
- That there are not cavemen existing somewhere?
- That dinosaurs still exist somewhere?
- That ghosts do not exist?
- That we all see the same thing in the same way?
- That we know what somebody means?

- That what we do is 'right'?
- That there is not a cure for old age?

Class book – Philosophy census (all ages)

You may also wish to compile the thoughts of parents and adults in a census home-school class book. Insert one question per double spread. Suggest that children and their parents choose one or more questions to answer. At the end of the project, send the list out as a questionnaire for families to complete together. It would be interesting to do this across the whole school and collect additional questions from children to add to the census.

 Children and parent/carer census questions

- Who has been the most important person in your life?
- What is the most valuable thing you have ever learned?
- What will be the best invention in your life time?
- What scares you most?
- What object would you save from a fire?
- What is your favourite smell?
- What message would you leave your great grandchildren?
- What would you have done differently?
- What changes can you make?
- What helps you sleep at night?
- What could you teach someone?
- If you had one rule everyone had to obey what would it be?
- What makes you laugh?
- What hope is there?
- How might mankind evolve?
- What object wouldn't you want to live without?
- What wouldn't you share?

Introducing philosophy journals

If you have received a positive reaction to the class journals, you may feel ready to start sharing the children's individual thinking journals with parents by sending them home. Parents will appreciate the fact that their opinions are valued too. It is important to commit to working with parents fully in order to gain their support. Parents must be made aware of how and why we do philosophy.

Send a short letter home explaining that you will be sending the books home to share after each philosophy session and that you would like them to be returned when completed on or before the following session.

Inside the front cover of the journals, you should stick an explanatory information sheet reminding parents what to do and what benefits P4C holds.

Each teacher writes his or her own slightly different version of the letter as we all have personal reasons why we feel it is integral to learning.

The following is the letter that I use and stick inside the front cover of the journals. You can find a template online to download and use if you wish.

What do we do in philosophy?

- We are shown a stimulus – it could be a story, a poem or piece of music. We might also use a photo, picture or object to look at.
- We draw a picture in our journal to explain what we think or what we want to find out.
- We then have some thinking time alone or in small groups to discuss our pictures or anything we are curious about in response to the stimulus.
  - o We think about the interesting philosophical themes of the stimulus.
- We ask interesting questions about the stimulus and the teacher records them on a large piece of paper.
- We look for connections and links between the questions.
- We might vote on the questions that most interest us or decide which one we want to discuss in our session.
- We discuss our thoughts and ideas about issues that arise from the questions. This is called a dialogue.
- We take a question that may have arisen from the session and write it in our journal to talk about with a grown-up at home. Any members of the family are invited to share their ideas as well.

Please take some time to think and talk together at home about the homework question. Please write down what your child thinks using his or her exact words and then write what the adults think too. Please return to school for the following week.

Thank you for your support.

[Class teacher name]

I also find it useful to send home a letter with the journal explaining why learning to think philosophically is so valuable. Here is an example below, which is also available on the companion website for you to use as a starting point.

What is your child learning?

- Philosophy taps into your child's curiosity through reasoning, problem solving, imagination and creativity.
- It develops their communication skills enabling them to articulate, listen and take turns.
- It teaches them the language of debate and how to make connections between statements.
- It helps them become more critical thinkers and question their own ideas as well as those of others in a non-threatening situation.
- It develops good relationships with their peers; they learn to work together to build on each other's ideas and thoughts.
- It teaches moral citizenship. They learn to take responsibility for their actions and views.
- It helps build self-confidence and self-esteem.
- Because there are no definite right and wrong answers, philosophy will challenge their thinking and they will want to share their thoughts with you and find out your opinions as well.
- The more a philosopher questions, the more they will want to find out.

When writing the set homework in the children's journals, always add a line that says 'child thinks because . . .' and 'adult thinks because. . . .' It is useful to have a template set up on the computer that you can change each week and print out to stick in the books. You could also give a slip of paper with the question on it for the children to stick in their books as well. In addition to writing up the points to consider on the parent's notice board, it is worth writing them in the journal for those parents who do not pick their children up or may not take the time to read it or remember it. This is especially useful in the early days of sending work home as you are modelling philosophical ways of thinking for parents. Below are a couple of examples of the homework questions pasted into the journal.

Example – Foundation stage (ages 4 and 5 years) in response to a philosophical discussion about what makes something artistic

What is art?

- If an elephant paints, is it art?
- If we spill a pot of paint by mistake is the result art?
- Can a baby be an artist?
- Is a pile of bricks art?

Example – Using a picture book for Key Stage 1 (ages 5–7 years)

This week, we have been thinking about *Aldo* by John Burningham.
    The little girl has an imaginary friend. The children's question is:

Was Aldo real?

Philosophical issues to consider

- How do we know if something is real?
- Where do our thoughts come from?
- Is there a difference between dreams and awake thinking?

Key Stage 2 journals

The following examples of homework questions that have been shared with parents have been contributed by some Year 5 pupils (ages 9 and 10 years) from North Lakes Primary School in Penrith.

Date: 28th March.

Due in: After Easter.

In school this term we are learning about respect for property and each other. We have also bee\n exploring thoughts and thinking on the Life Education Bus. This week I would like you to consider the following question:

What are Thoughts?

Points to consider: (These are just to give you some ideas – feel free to write about what you BELIEVE)

- When do we think?
- Why do we think?
- When you have had a thought, what do you usually do?
- What would happen if we didn't have any thoughts?

PLEASE GIVE EXAMPLES FROM YOUR OWN EXPERIENCE

CHILD THINKS...because...	ADULT THINKS...because...
Thoughts are when you think something in your brain. For an example, the teacher could give you a question and you think of the answer and that's a thought. Sometimes we have a special time to think and that's when we pray. We think because we have to make the right decisions and we think in school to get a good job. When I have had a thought I usually do it but sometimes if it's with another person I tell them and see if they agree. If we didn't have any thoughts we would all be quite dopey and we wouldn't be very clever enough to work.	People think all of the time really. It's hardly ever that you're just blank and not thinking about anything, even then you're probably miles away and thinking about all sorts without any effort. I've never really studied Psychology in great depth! But normal thoughts probably come into all different categories. You think about boring everyday stuff, but not in too much depth as it's not required. It takes some thought to get dinner sorted out, for example, although you're sort of on auto pilot then. Or you could have really important decisions you need to decide, and it's so complicated and required so much thought that you need to talk about it or write it down.

Sometimes when you're nearly asleep at night you have sort of pretend picture stories in your head about if something really brill happened, and sometimes you just think of bad things that have happened, and that's just a waste of time as it doesn't do anyone any good. |

Date: 27th November 2009

Due in: 4th December 2009

In out philosophy and thinking time this term, we have been discussing and exploring 'getting on a falling out'. This week I would like you to consider the following question:

Why do most people have friends?

Points to consider:

- What are friends?
- Why do we have friends?
- Do we always need our friends?
- Can you be happy without friends?

PLEASE GIVE EXAMPLES FROM YOUR OWN EXPERIENCE

CHILD THINKS...because...	ADULT THINKS...because...
• Friends are people who look out for you, play with you, have a laugh with you and cheer you up when you are glum.	• Friends are people you know well, people you trust, people you spend a lot of time with, people you share ideas and secrets with and people who you have fun with.
• We have friends to keep us joyful and happy, friends to stop us getting bullied and friends that share things in our lives like toys, games, privileges, time, money, food, activities and love.	• We have friends to reassure us, to help us, to praise us and to help us overcome difficulties. They are usually good listeners and trustworthy and reliable.
• We need our friends a lot of the time because they help to keep us happy and determined. However sometimes we have to do things on our own so that you can help to make yourself stronger and rely on yourself.	• Our friends help to keep us happy and it is better to be in a positive frame of mind rather than a negative one. However, a good friend will know when to take a back seat so that someone else can do a task by themselves or solve a problem alone in order to make themselves stronger for the experience.
• It would be very difficult to be happy without friends because there would be no-one there to help you when you are feeling down in the dumps or lonely or frightened.	• It would take a strong-minded individual or someone with a lot of self confidence to remain happy and to cope with all that life has to throw at people and do so without the support of at least one friend. However, sometimes people substitute friends for companions of an animal variety!

Date: 1st December

Due in: 8th December

In out philosophy and thinking time this term, we have been discussing and exploring 'getting on a falling out'. This week I would like you to consider the following question:

Are arguments ever good?

Points to consider:

- What is an argument?
- What can cause an argument?
- What do you usually argue about?
- Who do you usually argue with?

PLEASE GIVE EXAMPLES FROM YOUR OWN EXPERIENCE

CHILD THINKS...because...

- It is when two people (or more people) start getting angry at each other, because they don't agree on something. They also shout at each other.

- People disagreeing causes an argument. Arguments can be caused if people are lazy and don't do good work. Sometimes arguments start when people aren't very friendly with each other.

- My arguments are usually about my toys and who can play with them or borrow them. (However, I do share well.)

- Usually it is my sister (Maisie) when we can't agree on what to watch on TV. I also argue at times with my friends when they say I am no good at football and won't let me join in. I like football!

ADULT THINKS...because...

- An argument is normally a heated exchange of words when people strongly disagree on a subject. They can shout and scream at each other. Sometimes an argument can go too far and cause wars between countries. People can also resort to violence when an argument gets out of hand.

- Arguments can start over really small things. Children argue over silly things like sharing toys, wanting their own way, etc. Adults can argue over different ways of doing things. Sometimes resentment over other people's actions can cause a row. Arguing sometimes is a way of releasing pent up frustration and pressure.

- Sometimes I can argue about different things, usually it is if I feel that somebody isn't pulling their weight and I feel put on to do everything. I then like to have my say in a diplomatic way. I am probably more argumentative when I am tired and can't see straight. I am not a morning person so this is not a good time to wind me up.

- I wouldn't say that I argue a lot. I like to see them as disagreements. My husband doesn't argue back so this usually kills anything starting. My Grandmother is very argumentative, but I normally agree to disagree in this department.

With thanks to the class teacher and fellow SAPERE member Martyn Soulsby. The homework questions are again based on the dialogue and enquiry that the children have participated in. Martyn asks the children and parents for both honesty and examples from their experiences when considering their answers. This trust is of course something that has to be earned over time.

Does doing the right thing make you truly happy?

- If you have done the wrong thing, how do you feel?
- How do you know if it is the right or wrong thing to do?
- Have there been times when you have done the right thing but have felt sad?

If lots of people think something, does that mean they are right?

- How do we know if somebody is right?
- Should we always follow the opinions of others?
- Is it difficult to have a different opinion to someone else?

What would happen if no one were ever afraid?

- Is it possible to not be afraid of 'something'?
- What would happen if there was no such thing as fear?
- How would the place you live in and the people around you be different?

Is it better to follow or to lead?

- Is it easy to be a leader?
- Do you find it easy being told what to do?
- What do you do if you do not agree with the leader?

Reflective questions on home-school thinking

- How will you approach philosophical cohesion across the school community?

- Why is it important to involve parents?
- What problems might you anticipate in your setting and how might you overcome these?
- Why is the parent voice important?
- How can community input be maximized?
- How can you model philosophical rigour in home-school communication?

References

Browne, A. (1988), *Hansel & Gretel.* London: Red Fox.

— (1994), *Zoo.* London: Red Fox.

Burningham, J. (2000), *Aldo.* UK: Random House.

DFES (2007), *The Early Years Foundation Stage Every Child Matters: Play and Exploration.* UK: Crown.

McAfee, A. and Lewis, A. (1988). *Why Do Stars Come Out at Night?* London: Red Fox.

Paley, V. G. (1981), *Wally's Stories: Conversations in the Kindergarten.* Cambridge, MA: Harvard University Press.

Stanley, S. and Bowkett, S. (2004), *But Why?: Teacher's Manual: Developing Philosophical Thinking in the Classroom.* London: Network Educational Press.

Tickle, D. C. (2011), *The Early Years: Foundations for Life, Health and Learning.* UK: Crown.

Resources

Concept cards

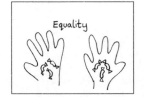

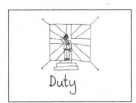

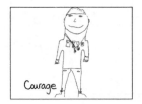

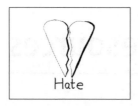

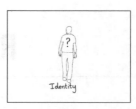

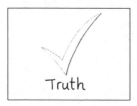

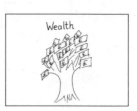

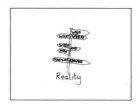

Same Different cards

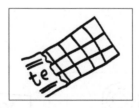

 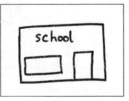 

The Philosophy Bridge

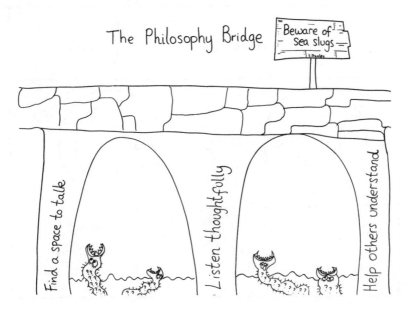

Jack and the Beanstalk handout

Choice card

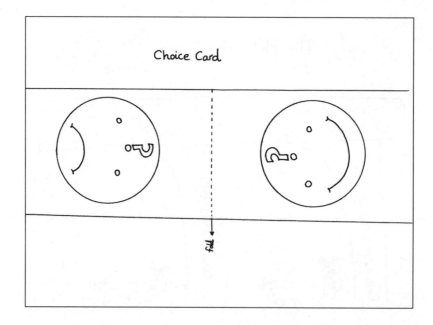

Index